Child
Development

D1027349

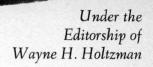

Under the
Editorship of
Wayne H. Holtzman

Child Development: The Human, Cultural, and Educational Context

W. H. O. SCHMIDT
University of Alberta

HARPER & ROW, PUBLISHERS
New York, Evanston, San Francisco, London

Sponsoring Editor: George A. Middendorf
Project Editor: Sandra G. Turner
Designer: Jared Pratt
Production Supervisor: Robert A. Pirrung

Child Development:
The Human, Cultural,
and Educational Context

Library of Congress Cataloging in Publication Data

Schmidt, W H O
    Child development.

    Bibliography: p.
        1. Child study. I. Title.
    [DNLM: 1. Child development. 2. Child psychology.
    WS105 S353c 1973]
    BF721.S446   155.4   73-7162
    ISBN 0-06-045781-3

To:
Ria,
Georg,
Graciela,
Bruno

Contents

6. Language, Cognition, and the Development of Intellectual Abilities   105

Foreword

When Professor Schmidt did me the honor of inviting me to write some introductory words to this book, I asked myself: Can a foreword really add anything of value? I had seen the manuscript at various stages of preparation, and I knew that the book would make its way on its own merits.

But when I saw the completed manuscript, I discovered in myself the pleasure of taking part again in an adventure, of joining an excellent scholar in opening ways of approaching and understanding the human child. Schmidt sees clearly that the child, though born in the most biological way, only "develops" into the *human* child thanks to education. "Education" is here understood in the comprehensive sense of upbringing, formation, and the child's participation in becoming himself—i.e., himself as an individual human person, as a fellowman in reciprocity with other people, as a member of a society and a participant in a particular culture. The young animal grows, but the child is humanized.

Of course, the biological conditions must be studied and respected. But then: Which conditions of humanization will be available? What will be offered to the child as an opportunity, as an aim? Which psychological processes, once started on these presuppositions, will develop? How will they be structured? What will be their content? How will they affect the child and in what kind of person will they result?

Schmidt's idea of the child included from the very beginning this reciprocity of child and education, child and world of experience, child as an active agent in relation to the world as well as to himself. Consequently, Schmidt sees the child *not* as a fact in itself, in a framework of biological and other "conditioning" forces isolated from itself, *but* as a unit of personal inventing, learning, and creativity *within* a unit of reciprocal production of a person and a structured mind, *within* a larger unit again of "culture." Thus, Schmidt sees the child as a *human* person in a human world. In this way, too, we now find our way from scientific categories of analysis to the human action of educating and growing up into somebody.

Schmidt goes straight toward the meeting-point with contemporary psychology and also informs the reader of alternative points of view; in this way he initiates the reader into the world of educational psychology of today.

This book offers the outcome of a cross-fertilization between European, American, and African contributions to the field of educational psychology. Schmidt is the exceptional scholar who lived and worked for many years in these three continents, a lifelong experience basic for his fundamental approach to the subject of this book.

M. J. LANGEVELD
Institute of Education
University of Utrecht, Holland

Preface

What today is called developmental psychology has undergone many metamorphoses since Jean-Jacques Rousseau wrote his *Émile* in the eighteenth century and introduced the notion of natural stages of development. Those metamorphoses reflect not only the impact of empirical observation and experimentation but, on occasion, massive shifts in the conceptual framework within which ontogenetic development is viewed. Jonas Langer, in *Theories of Development* (1969), looking at the present North American scene as well as casting some glances back into history, has classified developmental theories into three groups: the psychoanalytically oriented (Erikson's approach might be considered a prototype); mechanical-mirror theories—which, generally speaking, apply learning theories of the classical and instrumental conditioning type to the study of developmental phenomena and thus tend to obliterate the distinction between development and learning (Bijou and Baer, Bandura and Walters); and organic-lamp theories, which are heavily influenced by biological thinking (Piaget, Heinz Werner).

While all of these theories have educational implications, and it is certainly worthwhile and essential for any educational psychologist to search in these theories (and in the empirical findings resulting from research guided by them) for their educational implications, none of them assigns to the *phenomenon of education* a central place in the conceptualization of child development itself.

This book is an attempt to give the phenomenon of education a central place in conceptualizing child development and in interpreting some of the data about child development.

As I understand it, the message ethologists like Konrad Lorenz have for psychology is this: Before you start talking about learning and behavior, try to define the important species-specific characteristics of the species you are studying.

Among the species-specific characteristics of the human being, the one that stands out most clearly and is receiving increasing attention from developmental psychologists is the ability to symbolize. Cassirer has spoken of man as *animal symbolicum*, the being that symbolizes and creates symbolic worlds. Werner and Kaplan's *Symbol Formation* (1963), drawing as it does not only on recent experimental research but also on a vast European tradition of thinking about language and thought, is a landmark in developmental psychology in this respect. Joseph Church's *Language and the Discovery of Reality* (1962) placed language at the center of the description of cognitive development even before compensatory education and Head Start programs started putting such heavy emphasis on language development. To the publications of these authors I owe a great deal. My book also emphasizes language and speech (one form of symbolization, not the only one) and its ramifications in the total behavior and personality of the developing human being—especially in Chapters 4 and 6.

But there are other species-specific characteristics. The biologist Adolf Portmann has documented the view already expressed by Johann Gottfried Herder in the eighteenth century: The human infant is more helpless and, in proportion to the total life-span, is helpless over a longer period of time than the young of other species are; coupled with this, he shows greater plasticity. Ashley Montagu, in his book *The Direction of Human Development* (1956), attaches great importance to this. The implications of these characteristics (helplessness, plasticity), however, cannot be fully appreciated if viewed in isolation. Chapter 2 discusses the implications in relation to the symbolizing potentiality of the human being as well as in relation to another species-specific characteristic, which M. J. Langeveld first formulated in 1956 (*Studien zur Anthropologie des Kindes*); since then Langeveld has been frequently quoted in educational and psychological discussions in Europe: The child is an *animal educandum*—a being that not only can but *must* be educated in order to realize his potentialities as a human being.

To avoid the kind of misunderstanding that might easily arise from the multifocal and constantly shifting meaning of the word "education" in the English language, it should be made clear that education is not being identified with "schooling" such as has recently evolved in technological Western societies: The latter is a special case of the former. Jerome Bruner has written about this, and it has been the focus of some of my research. It is an important special case, worthy of more serious treatment than as just another environmental variable on a par with other variables that in some unspecified way might affect the course of human development or be affected by it. Much of Chapter 6 is devoted to the effect of schooling on development, a subject about which we can learn a great deal by looking at children in societies in which our type of schooling (Western European, North American) is something very new and sometimes very alien.

Education starts at birth, with the "primordial sharing" described by Werner and Kaplan; it continues as an interactional relationship between a more mature person (mother, father, adult, an ever-widening circle), who cares for the child and cannot escape his role as educator, and a less mature person (infant, child, young person), who attaches himself to the more mature person and inevitably is the educand (the one being educated). The educational relationship is a special form of a general human relationship. It can become institutionally elaborated and defined, and usually is, but it need not be so. We have no choice about educating and being educated (though we may educate badly and be badly educated): The biological givens (including what psychologists call *attachment behavior*) make education inevitable, and society does not condone extreme forms of educational neglect. There is no greater test of an adult's essential humanity than the way in which he enters into the educational relationship with a child. In his novel *Tell Me How Long the Train's Been Gone* (New York: Dial, 1968), James Baldwin, without using the word "education," has captured its very essence:

> If it is true, as I suspect, that people turn to each other in the hope
> of being created by each other then it is absolutely true that the
> uncreated young turn, to be created, toward their elders. Thus,
> whoever has been invested with the power of enchantment is guilty
> of something more base than treachery whenever he fails to exercise
> the power on which the yet-to-be-created, as helplessly as newborn
> birds, depend. Well, yes, I saw at last what was demanded of me.
> I would have to build a nest of materials I would simply have to

find, and be prepared to guard it with my life; and feed this creature and keep it clean and keep the nest clean; and watch for the moment when the creature could fly and force those frightened wings to take the air. [Pp. 82–83]

Taking wing, in the case of the human being, is not a single event but a series of diverse events over a period of many years. There have been great advances in the institutionalization and instrumentation of education; in my most pessimistic moments, I feel that there have been no advances in education itself. It is for this reason, I believe, that it is so desperately necessary to give the phenomenon of education a central place in our conceptualization of child development.

This book was written on three continents over a period of several years, and I am indebted to many people for helping me develop my own ideas. Most of all I am indebted to Professor M. J. Langeveld of Utrecht University in Holland, whose numerous contributions to the study of education and developmental psychology are well known in Europe and who is also a great human being. I have had many discussions with him, and without his encouragement and support I would hardly have completed the book. I owe a great deal also to my students, at both the senior undergraduate and graduate levels, to whom I have exposed my ideas and who have responded with understanding and quite often with excitement and a new involvement. I feel that I must mention six of my former students by name, because dialogue with them has in no small way helped me articulate various aspects of the conceptual framework presented in this book. Chanderpaul Ramphal carried out an investigation in South Africa in a community in which schooling was not compulsory and was able to show the impact of Western-type schooling on intellectual development. Five former students looked closely at the interpersonal matrix within which development (particularly cognitive development) takes place: Terence Hore and Paul Brady looked at mother-child interactions, Andor Tari investigated father-child relationships, Manjuli Gon investigated developmental changes in interpersonal perception, and Bruce Bain carried out a study of the ontogenetic development of participative perception and arrived at a tentative statement of a theory of perception at variance with that of Piaget.

In order to make the argument flow smoothly, comments and references are given at the end of each chapter; the reader may ignore them, but the serious student may find them valuable. Instead of the usual long and all-inclusive bibliography, a structured list of what I consider fundamental books (some of them old) is given. In addition, at the end of each chapter some topics are suggested for further exploration. It is hoped that the comments, structured bibliography, and topics for exploration will aid the serious student not just in understanding the ideas in the book but in developing them further. The aim of teaching, after all, is not to cover all the subject matter nor to provide final answers, but to lead the learner to ask significant questions and to make him independent of the teacher and able in his own turn to teach his students and educate the young.

W. H. O. SCHMIDT

Acknowledgments

Reprinted by permission of the publisher from John G. Navarra, *The Development of Scientific Concepts in a Young Child.* (New York: Teachers College Press; copyright 1955 by Teachers College, Columbia University).

Excerpted from *Metamorphosis* by Ernest G. Schachtel. Basic Books, Inc., Publishers, New York.

From *The New Mathematics and an Old Culture: A Study of Learning Among the Kpelle of Liberia* by John Gay and Michael Cole. Copyright © 1967 by Holt, Rinehart and Winston, Inc. Reprinted by permission of Holt, Rinehart and Winston, Inc.

Child
Development

CHAPTER 1

In Search of a Conceptual Framework for the Study of Child Development

Each current in psychology has its own implicit philosophy of man. Though not often stated explicitly, these philosophies exert their influence in many significant and subtle ways.[1]

Carl R. Rogers

About the origins of the study of child development M. J. Langeveld, the Dutch educationist and child psychologist, writes: "Compared with the ancient and honourable concern for the continuity of society and of culture, to which educators and didacticians as well as philosophers and politicians have devoted their attention since time immemorial, the psychology of the child is as young as a child."[2] It is indeed young. The empirical observation of children came into its own in the second half of the nineteenth century, though in the eighteenth century the question of how a child "develops" into an adult was already beginning to be asked. Why should this interest arise so late in history—for surely children, no less than society and culture, have been with us since time immemorial too?

SOCIOECONOMIC CHANGES AND CHILD STUDY

A full and definitive answer will not be attempted here. One factor, however, stands out very clearly: The interest in child development arose, and gained momentum, as the Industrial Revolution began to change radically the conditions under which people lived and children grew up. A temporary, and certainly grim, aspect of the Industrial Revolution (the exploitation of child labor in factories and mines) focused attention on the need for children to enjoy a sheltered and protected period of their lives in which they could grow to maturity. But much more important than this were the more permanent changes: Through the growth of medical science and consequent improvements in nutrition, there has been a phenomenal lengthening of the average life span; the demands of an increasingly differentiated and complex economic system, dependent on science and technology, became such that the period of preparation for the tasks of adulthood had to be prolonged considerably; the increase in overall wealth made possible the luxury of a longer period of sheltered childhood; eventually, compulsory schooling for all was introduced in the Western countries.[3] Adolescence, as a protracted period of development in which the individual is already physically and sexually mature while still not an adult with adult responsibilities and privileges, became a phenomenon sufficiently important to draw attention to itself only in the second half of the nineteenth century.[4]

Social and political ideas and realities also began to change. With some justification, it can be said that as long as the individual had little choice, or none at all, with regard to his future occupation and station in life, the problem of how a child developed into an adult was not a pressing one so far as either the individual or the needs of society was concerned. The fact that a child from the poorer classes occasionally showed striking intellectual potentialities, which with proper education might suit him for a station in life other than that of his father, was, as we know, always recognized by the church, which gave higher education to many such children;[5] but before the eighteenth century this did not lead to the fundamental question of the relationship between the development of children and the conditions in which they grow up. It was in the eighteenth century, with its strong interest in social and political reform culminating in the French Revolution, that attention was drawn to the relationship between the opportunities society makes available to children and the course their development would be likely to take.[6]

The empirical evidence for the assertions may have been lacking, but the questions were being asked and the ideas were being formulated. In the eighteenth and earlier centuries, the economic system was too undifferentiated to make available much choice of occupation to individuals; gradually, in the course of the nineteenth and twentieth centuries, one's choice of occupation became not only a privilege to be granted, however grudgingly, but a condition imposed by the diversification and differentiation of the economic system. Society began to be more and more interested in the potential abilities of children, which would make them suitable as adults to carry out the diversified, and increasingly specialized and complex, work it wanted done. Perhaps this did not represent an interest in the child as such, but the question of what a child is and what his potentialities are, and how the conditions, including his education, under which a child grows up affect the direction and course of his development, could no longer be avoided.

However, it is one thing to begin to see childhood and adolescence as phases in the development of the human being that demand and invite careful study and to see some sort of relationship between child development and the conditions under which the child grows up; it is quite another to acquire a conceptual framework within which to observe the child and to interpret the meaning of these observations.

THE INFLUENCE OF BIOLOGY

The conceptual framework within which much of the child psychology has attempted to interpret child development is a biological and evolutionary one. This trend started even before Darwin. We shall trace, very briefly, two strands in the history of this conceptual framework and indicate some of the problems it raises for our understanding of child development in an educational context.

The biological and evolutionary frame of reference is evident, for instance, in the great influence of animal psychology on child psychology and on the psychology of learning. It is evident, too, in the work of many psychologists, who do not themselves experiment with animals but employ concepts borrowed from biology and use them sometimes as analogies or metaphors and sometimes as statements implying a fundamental identity between the functions of psychological processes from amoeba to mollusc to man. One might think here of Piaget's use of the concepts of assimilation and accommodation to describe the function of intelligence at all levels of evolution.[7]

When Edward L. Thorndike was appointed to the chair of educational psychology at Teachers College, Columbia University, around 1900, his first great innovation was to study the learning processes of animals (mainly cats in puzzle boxes) in order to throw light on the learning processes of children and of human beings generally.[8] Rats, as is well known, have had to run through mazes in order to satisfy the curiosity of psychologists as to how learning occurs, and projections to human learning have been made on that basis. Köhler studied the intelligence of chimpanzees, and for many years after that time (1917) Köhler's experiments were included in many discussions of learning and problem-solving processes in children, the special point at issue being the nature of "insight."[9] Karl Bühler regarded the observations of Köhler as fundamental to an understanding of the intellectual development of children; in fact, for some unknown reason he spoke of Köhler as a *child* psychologist.[10]

Much more recently, Harlow has carried out fascinating work with monkeys on mother-child relationships, social development, conditions in which curiosity manifests itself, "learning to learn," and acquisition of "concepts," and all this is intended to throw light on human development as well.[11] A considerable amount of work by a number of investigators has been devoted to the study of the effects of sensory deprivation in young animals in order to understand better the effects of deprivation on cognitive development in children.[12] One could go on for a long time listing examples of the pervasive influence of the study of animal behavior on child psychology.

Now, undoubtedly the biological and evolutionary dimension is one aspect under which human development can and must be viewed, just as it can also be studied under the aspect of physiology or neurology or biochemistry. Nor is there any doubt that the biological and evolutionary framework has provided us with most important insights into human behavior. Investigation of developments and learning in animals other than man *is* important to our understanding of development and learning in human children, but the question is whether or not this is a sufficient frame of reference. What phenomena in child development do we tend to see when we adopt a biological frame of reference, and what tends to be left out? For it is clear that *any* conceptual framework makes us observe selectively and predisposes us to ask certain kinds of questions rather than others. This is not just a matter of "experimenter bias"; it is a matter of what one will choose as being worthy of investigation.

This does not mean that the child psychologist and the educational psychologist cannot learn anything from animal psychology; on the contrary, he can learn a great deal. It does mean, however, that he must have his own frame of reference, which enables him to assess what is relevant and in what way.

NATURAL DEVELOPMENT

The biological frame of reference can also be seen in the concept of natural development, which, going back as it does to the eighteenth century, antedates the theory of evolution and biology as we know these today but in a more modern version, seeks support from biology and physiology.[13]

Rousseau, a passionate critic of the society of his time—the second half of the eighteenth century—saw the possibility of reforming society, as so many critics of our present society do, in the education of children.[14] In his *Émile* he posits a *natural* development of the child, which must be protected against the influences of society so that the child can grow up as Nature intended him to be. Rousseau sees Émile as growing up not in the oversophisticated, corrupt, "unnatural" society of the eighteenth century but in a village in the south of France, where people are closer to the state of Nature, under the guidance of a tutor whose task is not to teach Émile but to enable Nature to do its work of teaching him. The assumption here is that there is a natural development on which we can rely and which will inevitably take place, provided we can keep in check the "unnatural" influences of society.

This is a powerful notion, one that has had a pervasive influence on child psychology. It was a good influence insofar as it led to observation of children in order to trace what was thought to be their natural development and thus led to greater recognition of the needs of children. It acted as a strong counterforce against the pressure of society, which in the course of industrialization in the nineteenth century and up to our time became ever more complex and demanding. Its influence was bad insofar as its romantic faith in the wisdom of Nature and its mistrust of Society led to over-simplification of the relationships between society, culture, and the development of the child.

The assumption of a natural development led, in the early part of the twentieth century, to an intense interest in the empirical study of the newborn child and the young infant in order to discover the "original nature" of man. "Original" is here seen as the earliest in time, before the child is influenced by "learning"; it is also seen as that which is "innate." The same Thorndike who turned to experimentation with animals in order to gain insight into the learning process entitled the first of his three volumes on educational psychology *The Original Nature of Man* and saw original nature in the context of the "nature versus nurture" controversy. With him, original nature was still significant in human development, though the influence of learning was carefully assessed and began to loom large.[15]

J. B. Watson, the founder of behaviorism, devoted much of his time to studying the behavior of newborn infants. With him, the notion of natural development completely disappeared; of course, there remains a process of physical and neurological growth. Taking over the concept of conditioning from Pavlov, he maintains that the human being grows into the sort of adult he becomes in the end as a result of processes of conditioning. In different words, Watson was repeating John Locke's (seventeenth century) notion of the mind as tabula rasa, a clean slate on which anything may come to be written. Such conditioning may be haphazard and unplanned, or it may be deliberate. It is not the infant's "original nature" that decides how he will develop but the process of conditioning to which he is exposed all the time. The wheel has turned full circle: With Rousseau, the child would develop naturally and in a way that would make him the shaper of a new and more natural society and culture if only Nature could be protected against the ravages of the present unnatural society; with Watson, the child's development is entirely in the hands of those who have the power to condition him and at the mercy of the unplanned conditioning to which he is exposed. The child in both cases is an object; it has no share in determining its own development.[16]

MATURATION VERSUS LEARNING

When "original nature" is seen as the nature that reveals itself at the beginning of a child's development, before learning has changed it, an important possibility has been overlooked—that what is given by nature may only mature and manifest itself at a later stage in the physical and mental growth of the child. Watson has been criticized for neglecting this possibility. The nature versus nurture controversy therefore had as a variant the "maturation versus learning" controversy, with many points of intersection between the two.

Arnold Gesell, who carried out his major empirical work in the 1920s but wrote some of his best-known books as late as the 1950s, is an example of a child psychologist who tried to see the development of the child as consisting mainly of a process of maturation, with the role of learning playing a supporting rather than an initiatory role. It is interesting to note how in his later publications he grappled with the problem of explaining how the child grows into a culture or, to use Gesell's term, becomes *acculturated*. However, Gesell's account of the acculturation process was less than satisfactory because his concept of culture was too simplistic.[17] This is what was meant when we said earlier that the romantic faith in the wisdom of Nature and the associated mistrust of Society led to oversimplification: In the post-Darwin era the romantic faith was transformed, in some writers, to a "scientific" faith in the biological impetus toward growth of the child. This concept distracted attention from an analysis of the real nature of society and culture, which was needed; moreover, it prevented the examination of the initiatory, rather than merely supportive, role of learning in child development.[18]

From this concept of maturation there emerged, as an implication for teaching, the concept of the "readiness" of the child for coping with specified learning tasks at school. The most frequently specified learning tasks have been the ones with which the child is confronted when he first enters school: learning to read and to deal with concepts of number. Of course, it was never asserted that learning had nothing at all to do with the child's readiness to cope with specified tasks, only that maturation was the fundamental factor and that the process of maturation could not be *appreciably* speeded up.

The concept "reading readiness" appears to have been introduced in the United States in a publication of the National Society for the Study of Education in 1925, though the notion that too-early learning of reading would lead to failure and/or would do irreparable harm had been expressed as early as 1896 by Patrick.[19] Carleton Washburne, with M. V. Morphett, provided the empirical facts that seemed to prove it was a waste of time (and probably harmful too) to try to teach children with a mental age lower than 6½ years, or at the very least 6 years, to read.[20] This was in 1929, and the investigation on which the finding was based was carried out in schools in Winnetka. With amazing regularity this finding was quoted as late as 1948 by authorities in the field of reading, even by eminent investigators into the problems of reading backwardness like Schonell, in order to warn against the danger of beginning too early with the teaching of reading.[21] However, an analysis of Morphett and Washburne's original paper reveals (even to a person with no sophisticated knowledge of statistical procedures) that their inferences were based on very scanty evidence indeed and that the generalization from the findings in Winnetka schools to schools where the age distribution of pupils and the conditions in which the teaching of reading takes place are very different rested on very insecure foundations. The investigation was undertaken in schools where the entrance age was so high that there were very few pupils with mental ages below 6 years, and the median age as well as the mode were in the region of 6½ years, the age found by Morphett and Washburne to be necessary for a child to be able to profit from formal reading instruction. It can be argued that the children with the lowest mental and/or chronological ages in any class will tend to have difficulties simply because in class teaching, particularly when fairly large numbers of children are involved, the teaching tends to be geared to the pace and learning ability of the average children in that class.[22] Nevertheless, the inference of Morphett and Washburne became a generalization and, in turn, a well-accepted dogma.

It is true that not all writers accepted the dogma. They were able to point out that in Scotland, for instance, children went to school at the age of 5 years and were subjected to formal instruction in reading as early as that with success. Emma A. Betts even called the notion that children could not profitably learn to read with mental age lower than 6 years a myth, basing her view not so much on experimental investigations as on her own observation of children in a great many classrooms.[23]

Why was the generalization of Morphett and Washburne accepted so readily and uncritically for such a long time? The explanation seems to be that it fitted in with basic preconceptions about the role of biologically determined maturation: the maturation of intelligence, which accounts for the link between reading readiness and mental age, and the maturation of perceptual abilities required in reading. The fear of doing harm by going against nature—an echo of Rousseau's notion of a natural development with which we must interfere as little as possible—was also evident. The possibility of *appreciably* influencing "readiness to read" by teaching and providing appropriate experiences seemed remote; the prereading activities included in well-known schemes of teaching reading, such as that of A. I. Gates, were intended for the child who is maturationally on the threshold of readiness for reading instruction.[24]

SPEEDING UP DEVELOPMENT

Today there is much evidence to indicate that when teaching methods and learning environments, including the learning environment in the home, are changed in appropriate ways, children turn out to be ready for reading at a much earlier age. The most dramatic evidence comes from such experiments as those being carried out on the use of a simplified alphabet (Initial Teaching Alphabet) in England, methods of teaching reading to 2- to 6-year-old children by means of "talking" typewriters being developed in the Human Response Laboratory at Yale by O. K. Moore, and Doman's widely publicized methods for teaching reading concurrently with the development of speech in the child.[25]

As regards the first of these experiments, it is not necessary to judge whether the results so far are due to the introduction of a new alphabet in the initial stages of learning to read or whether, as critics have suggested, they are due to other factors;[26] whatever the "cause," the results are still in the direction indicated. Nor are we here concerned with the question of whether children *should* be taught to read so much earlier but with the implications for the basic assumption concerning the role of maturation. The implication seems quite clear: By altering teaching methods and, more broadly and fundamentally, changing the conditions in which children have their experiences, one can affect the development of a child profoundly.

Similar implications emerge from recent experiments in the teaching of mathematics; in the United States, the U.S.S.R., England, and Europe, evidence is accumulating that children can deal with highly abstract concepts and principles at a much earlier age than was hitherto believed possible, provided the right approach is found in teaching.[27] J. S. Bruner's working hypothesis that "any subject can be taught at any stage of development" is certainly overoptimistic and overgeneralized, but it indicates clearly the shift in interpretation of "readiness for learning" and the role of maturation: Teaching, and the resultant learning, is held to be capable of speeding up appreciably the process of development of intellectual abilities.[28] A well-known monograph in a series published by the Institute of Education of the University of London has the title *The Bearings of Recent Advances in Psychology on Educational Problems;* the time seems ripe for a monograph that inverts that title to read *The Bearings of Recent Advances in Education on Psychological Problems.*[29]

There are many other aspects of the maturation-learning relationship on which we cannot touch here; a very basic discussion of the issues is given by Vygotsky.[30]

BIOLOGY AND EDUCATION

We must now summarize the main implications of the study of child development within a biological framework:

1. If the child psychologist and the educational psychologist turn to the study of animal behavior and development, they will not only have to look for identities and continuities but also to contrast, and they will have to pay attention not only to differences in complexity but also to differences in kind. Language, for instance, is not just an infinitely more complex means of communication than those available to animals; in some respects it is fundamentally different in kind.[31] The fact that a human child does not merely have to adapt to life in a natural environment and a social group but discovers a preexistent language and becomes a participant in a culture, which itself is essentially influenced by the use of language, not only complicates his socialization but also adds dimensions of existence that are fundamentally different in kind from those experienced by other animals.[32] About these animal psychology can tell us nothing.

2. If learning proves to be overwhelmingly important in the development of the child, then such development will have to be seen always in the concrete context of the child's interaction with other human beings, with things, and with the language and culture within which he creates his own world of meaning—and with that his own personality. Among the interactions with other human beings, there is one that deserves special attention, namely, that between the adult who educates and the child who is being educated. It is for this reason that the subtitle of this book includes reference not only to the human and cultural context but specifically also to the educational one.

The use of the term *education* requires some comment, because we may appear to be violating ordinary English usage. We have come to identify education with schools and schooling. Indeed, most books on "education" deal with what goes on in schools or what ought to go on there. However, the school is only a particular institutionalization of an important part of education in our highly scientifically oriented technological societies. The school has grown from the modest institution it was in the nineteenth century, with limited functions, to one that is blamed for all the ills of society and seen as potentially capable of curing them. It has extended (some would say overextended) its reach and therefore is exceedingly vulnerable to criticism. The radical critics of our schools, who go so far as to recommend the "deschooling of society," may be wrong in some of their diagnoses, but at least they are reminding us that the whole of education does not, and need not, take place in the school. Indeed, a great deal of education goes on already in the relationship between parent and child, before the TV set, and in community settings.

In this book, when we speak of the educational context we mean not only instruction or teaching, or "education within the narrow confines of the school," though it includes these too. Indeed, in Chapter 6 we shall examine the influence of schooling on cognitive development. Nor shall we deal with alternatives to schools as we know them today. Instead, we shall define the educational process simply as the interaction between an educator (adult) and an educand (child). This is not to deny that every institutional setting has its own built-in constraints and possibilities for affecting that educator-educand relationship, but to deal with these problems would require a book in itself. In discussing the development of the child, we shall focus our attention on the educand in this *reciprocal* relationship. We must do this with that reciprocity in mind, for without the educator the development would not be the same. How adults see children, what their feelings are about them, how much room for autonomy and for exercise of personal freedom and choice they leave to the child, what expectations they have of their children, what models they provide—these are just a few of the obvious ways in which the fate of the child is linked to what the educator feels, thinks, and does.

Educators are not only teachers. The human relatedness of a mother with *her* child, a father with *his* child, and a teacher with the children *in his or her care* and for whom he or she, in the literal meaning of the word, cares, is the basic "given" to which we must devote our attention. Only then are we able to see the biologically rooted process of maturation in a light that can reveal the educational dimension that transforms and gives meaning and direction to the child's biological growth processes and enables the *child himself* to give meaning to the world that impinges on him and to transform it, or some part of it, into *his* world.

In the next chapter we shall look at this educational dimension, which is present in all human development.

*Topics for
Further Exploration*

1.   At the beginning of this chapter, we mentioned social and economic changes since the eighteenth century that changed the conditions under which children grow up. With urbanization and birth control, the nuclear family has replaced the extended family system. From the point of view of the child's welfare, what do you see as the strengths and weaknesses of the small nuclear family?

2.   Read the Earl of Shaftesbury's speech to the House of Commons (England) on June 7, 1842, entitled "Children in Mines and Collieries," in William Kessen, *The Child* (New York: Wiley, 1965). We do not have those forms of child-labor exploitation today. What forms of child neglect and cruelty to children do we find today?

3.   There is a great deal of concern today about speeding up the cognitive development of children, starting even with stimulation of infants in the crib. What has brought about this concern? Is it justified? Are there dangers?

References and Comments

1.   C. R. Rogers, "Towards a science of the person," in *Behaviorism and Phenomenology—Contrasting Bases for Modern Psychology*, ed. T. W. Wann (Chicago: University of Chicago Press, 1964), p. 129.

2.   M. J. Langeveld, *Studien zur Anthropologie des Kindes*, 3d ed. (Tübingen: Max Niemeyer Verlag, 1968), p. 10.

3.   Philippe Aries, *Centuries of Childhood: A Social History of Family Life* (New York: Knopf, 1962). First published in French in 1960. Aries discusses the history of the distinctions we make (infant, child, adolescent, youth, young adult, etc.) in child development and shows how flexible these terms have been and how changes in usage reflect changes in social conditions. In the Middle Ages and right into the seventeenth century, a person of low social status was treated as a "child" regardless of his age, for he was regarded as

"dependent"; one left "childhood" (i.e., one's state of dependency) only by achieving a superior social or economic position. It was only among the upper classes that being a child or not being a child came to be linked with physical growth and physical characteristics. In the upper classes, for example, we find child marriage as a legal arrangement, but in all classes the lives of children and adults were hardly separated. Very young boys served in the army and navy; very young children were confronted with sex and death. As regards compulsory education, which so radically alters the conditions under which children grow up, we have to remind ourselves again and again that in most countries of the world it does not exist even today and that in Western countries it was introduced relatively recently. Even in England, for instance, it was introduced only in 1870; and it needed Lord Sandon's Act of 1876, prohibiting the employment during school hours of children under 10 years of age who lived within 2 miles of a school, to make compulsory education a reality for all children up to the age of 10 years. See also S. J. Curtis, *History of Education in Great Britain*, 5th ed. (London: University Tutorial Press, 1963).

4. Although child psychology emerged in Germany with Wilhelm Preyer (*Die Seele des Kindes*, 1882; English translation, *The Mind of the Child—The Senses and the Will*, 1903), Stanley G. Hall, the father of the child-study movement in the United States, is generally credited with first having focused on the study of adolescence. His monumental work, *Adolescence: Its Psychology and Its Relation to Physiology, Anthropology, Sociology, Sex, Crime, Religion and Education*, 2 vols. (New York: Appleton), appeared in 1904. See also J. H. van den Berg, *The Changing Nature of Man* (New York: Norton, 1961).

5. For a few details see G. M. Trevelyan, *English Social History* (London: Longmans, 1942), p. 75 (on the fifteenth century), p. 363 (on the eighteenth century).

6. See P. H. Idenburg, "The Ideal of Equal Opportunity," in *Education and Our Expanding Horizons*, eds. R. G. MacMillan, J. W. Macquarrie, and P. D. Hey, (Pietermaritzburg: Natal University Press, 1962), pp. 109–119.

7. The most comprehensive account of Piaget's work, from the early 1920s to about 1962, has been given by John H. Flavell in *The Developmental Psychology of Jean Piaget* (Princeton, N.J.: Van Nostrand, 1963). From a preface to the book written by Piaget him-

self, it becomes clear that Piaget regards Flavell's account as not doing justice to the basic theoretical (epistemological) issues underlying all his experimentation with children. The basic theoretical issues, and the philosophical tradition that provides the context for Piaget's views, is best dealt with by Hans Furth in his book *Piaget and Knowledge* (Englewood Cliffs, N.J.: Prentice-Hall, 1969). On the issue of maturation versus learning and for a very critical view of Piaget, see G. A. Kohnstamm, *Piaget's Analysis of Class Inclusion: Right or Wrong?* (The Hague: Mouton, 1967).

8. Thorndike's justification for this innovation is stated very simply in the second of his three volumes, entitled *Educational Psychology*, vol. II: *The Psychology of Learning* (New York: Teachers College, Columbia University, 1921): "The complexities of human learning will in the end be best understood if at first we avoid them, examining rather the behavior of the lower animals as they learn to meet certain situations in changed, and more remunerative, ways" (p. 6). This sounds sensible and practical, but the controversy about applying the results of experiments on animal learning to human learning has continued right up to our time, and there has been much disillusionment, particularly among educationally oriented psychologists, about the "practical" implications. There are two points to be made: (a) Thorndike's statement amounts to creating intuitively a model of learning based on processes in animals that we can only presume are learning processes because we know vaguely from our own experience what learning is. Consequently, Thorndike's model is based on intuition and circular reasoning. This would be a criticism coming from a nonbehavioristically oriented psychologist. (b) A great deal depends on which of the "lower" animals in the phylogenetic scale are chosen for learning experiments and to what extent species-specific characteristics are taken into account in interpreting what is to be considered as learning. This would be a criticism coming from biologists. For a discussion of this point, see W. Hodos and C. B. G. Campbell, "Scala Naturae: Why There Is No Theory in Comparative Psychology," *Psychological Review* 76 (1969): 337–350.

9. W. Köhler, *The Mentality of Apes*. First published in 1925; now available in Penguin Books, 1957.

10. See Langeveld, op. cit., p. 24.

11. For brief accounts of some of Harlow's work on the effects of different kinds of mother-infant relationships on the development

of young monkeys, see Harry F. Harlow, "The Nature of Love," *American Psychologist* 13 (1958):673–685, and, by the same author, "The Heterosexual Affectional System in Monkeys," *American Psychologist* 17 (1962):1–9. Harlow's work on "learning to learn" is described by McV. Hunt in his book *Intelligence and Experience* (New York: Ronald, 1961), pp. 77–83, where references to the publications of Harlow and his associates will also be found; some of the experiments originally designed for monkeys have been carried out with young children as well.

12. See D. O. Hebb, *A Textbook of Psychology* (Philadelphia and London: Saunders, 1958), chap. 6.

13. See W. Kessen, *The Child* (New York: Wiley, 1965).

14. J. J. Rousseau, *Émile*, trans. Barbara Foxley (London: Dent, 1963). Rousseau was deeply influenced by Buffon's *Natural History* and frequently quotes him. See for comparison and contrast a modern author like Ashley Montagu, *The Direction of Human Development* (London: Watts, 1957); behind the question of what man is like *by nature*, there is also a strong reforming zeal born out of a deep concern for the condition of man in the twentieth century, which has seen human aggressiveness on a scale that threatens to destroy mankind.

15. E. L. Thorndike, *Educational Psychology*, 3 vols: *The Original Nature of Man*, vol. 1, 1913; *The Psychology of Learning*, vol. 2, 1913; *Mental Work and Fatigue and Individual Differences and Their Causes*, vol. 3, 1914 (New York: Teachers College, Columbia University). Thorndike makes a distinction between "natural" and "original," and shows that what we commonly mean by "natural interests of children," for instance, is something that is largely acquired or learned. See vol. 1, p. 293: "The so-called 'natural' proclivities of man represent enormous changes from his 'original' proclivities. The effects of learning are as surely present in the common liking of boys for hunting, fishing, adventure and sport in the present senses of these words, as in their rare liking for geometry, computation and grammatical precision . . . the majority of the so-called 'natural' interests are largely acquired. —The doctrine that the 'natural' is the good, and should be the aim of education, is then very different from the doctrine that *original* nature is right. . . . It amounts roughly to declaring that the mixed product of original nature and the unconscious tuition of common circumstances and customs has ultimate value. That is false. Equally false is the doctrine that the 'natural' is essentially evil."

16. John B. Watson, *Psychology from the Standpoint of a Behaviorist* (Philadelphia: Lippincott, 1919). His book *Psychological Care of Infant and Child* (London: Allen and Unwin, 1928), written together with Rosalie Watson, shows us what kind of conditioning he favors in the early development of the child: "Treat them as though they were young adults. Dress them, bathe them with care and circumspection. Let your behavior always be objective and firm. Never hug them and kiss them, never let them sit on your lap. If you must, kiss them once on the forehead when they say goodnight. Shake hands with them in the morning. Give them a pat on the forehead if they have made an extraordinarily good job of a difficult task" (p. 73). He appears to be particularly afraid of too close a relationship between mother and child, for he recommends that mothers should sometimes leave their infants for some weeks so that they will not become too dependent on them. For the opposite view, showing the dangers of separation, see John Bowlby, *Child Care and the Growth of Love* (Baltimore: Pelican, 1953).

17. Arnold Gesell and Francis L. Ilg, *Infant and Child in the Culture of Today* (New York: Harper & Row, 1943).

    Arnold Gesell, *The First Five Years of Life* (New York: Harper & Row, 1940).

    Arnold Gesell and Francis L. Ilg, *The Child from Five to Ten* (New York: Harper & Row, 1946).

    Arnold Gesell et al., *Youth: Years from Ten to Sixteen* (New York: Harper & Row, 1956).

    Arnold Gesell and Catherine S. Armatruda, *Developmental Diagnosis*, 2d ed. (New York: Medical Department of Harper & Row, 1969).

    The critical remark about Gesell's concept of acculturation should not blind us to the immense value of Gesell's systematic observation of the development of American middle-class children, especially infants. His developmental tests for preschool children, with norms based on his observations, have proved most valuable in the assessment of infants' development. But because he has not concerned himself with children from *different* social classes and cultures, his concept of culture remains vague and the concept of maturation has to explain too much. The younger the child and the less he has been exposed to "the culture," the more convincing Gesell's observations are.

18. C.f., e.g., W. C. Olson, *Child Development* (Boston: Heath, 1949).

On p. 380: "The general philosophy (i.e., of "growth") as applied to the growing child is a simple one—each child is to be assisted in growing according to his natural design without deprivation or forcing in an environment and by a process which also supply a social direction to his achievement." The emphasis is on "growth," "natural design," and "social direction"; all this could be said about baboons as well—what about the culture?

19. C. T. W. Patrick, *Should Children Under Ten Learn to Read and Write?* (Iowa: University of Iowa, 1896). Only a little later, we find Hall (see note 4) arguing that the school entrance age should not be lower than 8 years: "Rousseau would leave pre-pubescent years to nature and to these primal hereditary impulsions and allow the fundamental traits of savagery their fling till twelve. Biological psychology finds many and cogent reasons to confirm this view if only a proper environment could be provided. . . . We should transplant the human sapling, I concede reluctantly, as early as eight, but not before, to the schoolhouse with its imperfect lighting, ventilation, temperature. We must shut out nature and open books" (pp. x, xi).

20. M. V. Morphett and C. Washburne, "When Should Children Begin to Read?" *Elementary School Journal* 31 (1931):496–503. Reprinted in *Readings in Child Psychology*, ed. Wayne Dennis (Englewood Cliffs, N.J.: Prentice-Hall, 1951), pp. 595–602.

21. F. J. Schonell, *Backwardness in the Basic Subjects*, 4th ed. (Edinburg and London: Oliver & Boyd, 1948, reprinted several times), see p. 186.

22. W. H. O. Schmidt, "An Investigation to Determine the Optimum Mental Age for Commencing Reading Instruction Under Conditions at Present Obtaining in Certain Schools in Pietermaritzburg and in Durban," *Journal of Social Research*, Pretoria (June 1955).

23. Quoted by W. B. Inglis, "The Early Stages of Reading: A Review of Recent Investigations," in *Studies in Reading: Publications of the Scottish Council for Research in Education* (London: University of London Press, 1949), p. 73.

24. Note, however, that Gates does not believe we can lay down a particular mental age for beginning to read; the mental age, in his view, must be related to the particular program of reading instruction the child is to follow. See A. I. Gates, "The Necessary Mental Age for Beginning Reading," *Elementary School Journal* 37 (March 1937): 497–508.

25. See J. Downing, *The I.T.A. Reading Experiment* (London: Evans Brothers for the University of London Institute of Education, 1964). *Educational Research* 6 (November 1963) contains three papers— by A. E. Sanderson, R. Lynn, and John Downing—on reading readiness. John Downing's paper also refers specifically to the work of Moore. See also G. Doman, *How To Teach Your Baby To Read* (New York: Random House, 1964).

26. See Vera Southgate, "Approaching I.T.A. Results with Caution," *Educational Research* 7 (1965):83–96.

27. The importance of the proviso "provided the right approach is found in teaching" cannot be emphasized too strongly. To drive home this point, I can think of no better paper than that of Max Wertheimer: "The Area of the Parallelogram," chap. 1 of his book *Productive Thinking*, enl. ed. (New York: Harper & Row, 1959). (The first version of this book appeared in German as early as 1925 under the title *Drei Abhandlungen zur Gestalttheorie, Erlangen*.) This deals with a "traditional" topic in geometry—not with the New Mathematics—and shows how, with the right approach, quite young children can understand what is involved. For a critical note on some of the recent optimism as to what children can learn, see Bernard Z. Friedlander, "A Psychologist's Second Thoughts on Concepts, Curiosity, and Discovery in Teaching and Learning," *Harvard Educational Review* 35 (1965):18–38.

28. J. S. Bruner, *The Process of Education* (Cambridge, Mass.: Harvard University Press, 1960; paperback, Vintage, 1963).

29. University of London Institute of Education, *Studies in Education*, no. 7 (London: Evans Brothers, 1955).

30. L. S. Vygotsky, "Learning and Development," *Educational Psychology in the U.S.S.R.*, ed. B. Simon, trans. Joan Simon (Stanford, Calif.: Stanford University Press, 1963).

31. See D. McNeill, *The Acquisition of Language* (New York: Harper & Row, 1970), chap. 3. See also R. A. Chase, "Evolutionary Aspects of Language," in *The Genesis of Language*, eds. F. Smith and G. A. Miller (Cambridge, Mass.: M.I.T. Press, 1966), pp. 253–268.

32. See Chapter 4.

CHAPTER 2

The Child as
Animal
Educandum

*The organic potentialities do not develop at all in the absence of
environmental influences. This is true of physical potentialities;
it is even more true of mental ones. The development of the mental
potentialities presents virtually infinite possibilities under the
action of varying environments. . . .*[1]

    M. F. Ashley Montagu

The term *animal educandum* was introduced by M. J. Langeveld,
who for a long time has been concerned with developing an
"anthropology of the child."[2] Lately there have been publications
by other educational theorists on the same theme.[3] What is meant
by this?

ANTHROPOLOGY OF THE CHILD

Anthropology in its widest sense simply means the study of man.
This can have different aspects: social, physical, psychological, and
philosophical. *Philosophical anthropology* (a term used quite widely
in Europe) is concerned with conceptions of man, both historical
and contemporaneous. Such conceptions are often implicit rather than
explicit; therefore they have to be articulated, compared, and clarified.
For instance, what are the conceptions of man and of children in the
writings of Freud or Skinner or Rogers?

    When we study child development we are concerned with em-
pirical observation; and, of course, we want to be able to use the
knowledge thus gained to help and educate children. But the

empirical facts themselves demand that we reflect on the implications for our basic conception of what a human being is and, more particularly, of what a child is *before* he is an adult human being. The anthropology of the child (in Langeveld's sense) deals with conceptions and assumptions concerning the "child in the process of becoming." Such reflection is not a substitute for the detailed empirical observation of behavior. However, it sets the stage for empirical observation, and it influences our interpretation of what we see.[4]

The plasticity of the human being described in the opening quotation is today widely recognized. Study of children in widely differing cultures has shown that what in one culture is regarded as a typical form of behavior, or a typical characteristic of children at certain ages, may be entirely missing in another.[5] The kind of personality that emerges when adulthood is reached may vary considerably, and there appears to be a relationship between the adult personality and child-rearing practices.[6] The conception of the kind of behavior of which an adult *should* be capable helps to form the personality pattern that emerges. Even what seems to be a purely biologically determined ability in infanthood, such as the age at which a child learns to sit upright or begins to walk, is to some extent subject to cultural differences.[7]

The term *animal educandum* implies more than that the child, by virtue of his plasticity, is educable; it implies that the child is a being that *must* be educated. There are two aspects to this. The one concerns his *humanization*, his development into a specifically human being with human characteristics. The other concerns his development as an individual person who needs educational help within the matrix of the specific society and culture into which he is born. He needs this in order to create for himself a meaningful life in commitment to, but not enslavement to, his own society and culture. (Note that this last statement implies a conception of the child as a being that "ought" to be granted a great deal of autonomy.)

Ashley Montagu has formulated a similar conception. Out of deeply felt concern for the future of mankind, which in the twentieth century has so abundantly demonstrated its competitive, aggressive, and destructive potentialities, he started to ask the questions: How do human beings become as they are? Are they "by nature" competitive, aggressive, and destructive? Were Thomas Hobbes and Sigmund Freud right in taking a pessimistic view of human nature, emphasizing man's aggressive tendencies as part of his instinctual equipment?[8] Can man be changed? What is "human" about being a human being? His book *The Direction of Human Development*[9] tries to answer these questions. It analyzes the implications of numerous empirical facts taken from biology, anthropology, social psychology, and early child development in order to find an answer. Ashley Montagu's first concern is man's socialization, but this broadens out into the question of the role of education in the formation of human personality, and a number of his essays and books deal with the latter.[10]

Ashley Montagu stresses the inadequacy of a purely biological interpretation of human development: "First, then, it should be said that no organism of the species so prematurely named *Homo sapiens* is born with human nature. Being human is not a status *with* which but *to* which one is born. Being human must be learned." Later in the same book, entitled *On Being Human*, he says: "On the basis of his obvious physical characteristics man is described as a mammal of the order *Primates*, genus *Homo*, and species *sapiens*. But what of his psychological classification? While every creature that is classified physically as man is thereby called *Homo sapiens*, no such creature is really *human* until it exhibits the conduct characteristic of a human being."

What then of the newborn infant? Is it not human? Ashley Montagu adds: "One can no more deny the status of being human to a newborn baby because it cannot talk, than because it cannot walk erect." He reconciles this with his previous statement by pointing to the promise the child shows of being able to develop the conduct characteristic of human beings: "The wonderful thing about a baby is its *promise*, not its performance—a promise to perform *under certain auspices*" (italics added).[11] Under certain auspices: The development of *Homo sapiens*, however great the promise may be, into a human being with conduct characteristic of human beings requires more than just being kept alive physically.

When Ashley Montagu speaks of the promise the human being shows, he is thinking specifically of a number of comparisons that have been made between the development of the child and that of the young of our nearest relatives, biologically speaking—the great apes. The work of Wolfgang Köhler, Robert W. Yerkes, and the Kelloggs is relevant.[12] He sums up one aspect of these studies in a brief sentence: "juvenile apes can do a great deal more than can a juvenile human, but the promise of the child far exceeds that of the brightest of apes."[13]

PRIMATE STUDIES OF LANGUAGE DEVELOPMENT

To be more concrete and specific, let us turn to a study (similar to that of the Kelloggs) of an ape reared as a human child, the experiment described by Cathy Hayes in her book *The Ape in Our House*.[14] It tells how a chimpanzee is reared from birth up to the age of 4 years under conditions approximating as closely as possible those in which a human child is raised. Its great advantage over the earlier experiment by the Kelloggs is that, whereas their experiment ended when the ape was 19 months old (a time when, in the human child, great developments normally begin in the sphere of language), Cathy Hayes' experiment continued until the ape, named Viki, was 4 years old.

Viki was raised among conditions closely approximating those in which a human child grows up, including a large measure of affection and security; much contact and interaction with the "parents," particularly the "mother"; opportunities to play, to go out, and to receive guests; and the sorts of toys and books a human child would have. Over and above these activities, a special program was developed to teach Viki to speak.

On developmental tasks designed and standardized for human children, the chimpanzee's performance in nine out of ten areas of development tested at just over 3 years of age, compared favorably with that of the child population on which the test was standardized. In fact, the chimpanzee's performance was above the average for human children. The ability of the chimpanzee to solve problems at the perceptual and motor level (that is, when objects were placed before her or were perceptually accessible) was particularly well developed, as evidenced not only by the special tests given to her but also by a number of incidents such as escaping from a yard surrounded by electrified wires.[15]

In the tenth area tested—language—however, we find a zero score, despite the fact that the animal learned to respond to a few "words." In the long run it is language that will enable the average child, and even a relatively dull child, to outstrip the chimpanzee in problem-solving ability. Much more significant than this ability is that language will open up a world of human meaning that nothing can open up for the chimpanzee—a point we shall develop in Chapter 4.

Other significant points of comparison are as follows. A child at the age of 3 to 4 years can already use language to transform his fantasies and to give expression to and elaborate on them, and he can indulge in make-believe; the chimpanzee, in an amazing episode described in the book, shows evidence of also being able to indulge in illusory play—for a while she plays with an imaginary pull-toy, but this is very transitory, ends in panic, and never reappears. The child at this age already relates past and future events to his own individual existence; he can remember and anticipate important events in his own life history. For instance, he can say: "Last birthday I was 3 years old; on my next birthday I will be 4 years old" in a way that is meaningful to him. An attempt to make Viki anticipate her birthday demonstrated her complete lack of the time dimension; a human child would already be beginning to live his own personal life, of which he would become aware reflectively.

Here, then, in language and the world of human meaning contained in it and accessible through it, in fantasy and imagination aided by language, in self-awareness and awareness of one's own past and projection into one's own future, lies some of "the promise of the child (that) far exceeds that of the brightest of apes."

More recent attempts to teach chimpanzees human language do not change the picture much. In these attempts a clearer distinction is made between language and vocal speech. Human language is tied to auditory input and output. What if we substitute for the auditory mode a visual one? Gardner and Gardner have used deaf-mute signs with a chimpanzee named Washoe.[16] At 25 months of age, Washoe had a vocabulary of 25 words and combined them spontaneously.

Was this the beginning of generating sentences? McNeill does not doubt that Washoe was using words to *refer* to events, but he suggests that Washoe's combinations of words do not fall into the patterns that have been observed in the case of human children when they move from the one-word utterance to two- and three-word utterances. He sees them as "unintegrated sequences of words, produced perhaps in the order of their importance to Washoe, but between which there are no grammatical relations."[17]

Premack has carried out an experiment with a chimpanzee named Sarah. He substituted plastic chips of varying colors and shapes for words. Instead of asking whether a chimpanzee would be able to acquire human language, he broke down the task into simple units and asked: Which of four major functions of language could a chimpanzee be taught? The functions he chose were: word, sentence, question, and metalanguage. Metalanguage is used in speaking *about* language. It is involved, for instance, in the simple statement "X is *the name of* Y." After 2 years of training, Sarah had a vocabulary of 80 words, including names, words for a variety of foods and objects, words for colors, and verbs, adjectives, and adverbs. Though Premack admits that it is difficult to prove competence in syntax, he does believe Sarah became "competent to some degree in the sentence function of language." She also learned the interrogative function; she understood and was able to pose questions. Finally, Premack presents evidence to show that the chimpanzee "thinks of the word not as its literal form (blue plastic) but as the thing it represents (red apple)."[18] No doubt there is room for argument about some of Premack's inferences, but the results are nevertheless impressive.

But what do these results prove? With regard to the acquisition of human language, the gap between the child and the chimpanzee is still a very wide one. Indeed, it cannot be otherwise, because the communication systems of different species of animals are species-specific and adapted to their *own* experiental worlds. However much the experiential world of the chimpanzee removed from its own kind and habitat and reared by humans may share with that of the human being, the two worlds remain far apart. Chase, referring to the work of Altmann, Marler, Tinbergen, and others, describes some of the communication systems of other species and makes the point that "the productive features of animal communication systems are specifically suited to quantitative and qualitative, species-specific requirements for information exchange."[19] In some species there are only tactile and chemical communication systems. In many, sound utterances play an important role, but no verbal-linguistic system is developed. The human being also communicates in nonverbal and nonauditory ways —through touch, gesture, facial expressions, glances, movement, posture, and so on. But in addition he has developed a verbal-linguistic communication system of singular power. We shall come back to this point in Chapter 4.

CHILDREN RAISED IN ISOLATION

The chimpanzees just described were compared with children who have grown up under normal conditions—the "certain auspices" to which Ashley Montagu refers: the fellowship of human beings and the care of adults. What happens when, in the development of the child, these auspices fall away? We can look now, as both Montagu and Langeveld do and many social psychologists have done, at some of the reported cases of children growing up in complete or near-complete isolation from other human beings.

Accounts of children reared in complete isolation from other human beings have long excited the imagination. At the time of Linnaeus (eighteenth century), who listed *Homo ferus* as a sub-division of *Homo sapiens*, nine historical records of "wild men" were available. Since then some 20 or more cases of such persons have been reported. Within the class of "feral man," we must distinguish between cases of children who have at some early stage been separated from human beings and have survived alone, and those who have grown up with animals. We shall look at one famous example of each and then turn to cases of a third type, namely, children who have grown up with minimal human interaction.

In the late eighteenth century, J. M. G. Itard reported on the case of a boy who was found in a forest completely naked, gathering acorns and roots to eat, and was eventually captured and brought back to civilization. The boy was given the name Victor and is often referred to as the Wild Boy of Aveyron. Itard describes the behavior of the boy and his own efforts to teach him to do the things ordinary human beings do, including speaking and reading.[20] The boy was then 11 or 12 years of age, and it could not be determined at what age he had started living in the forest in isolation from human beings or what the circumstances of his eviction from human society had been. Contrary to the expectations of those who took literally the notion of natural development, Victor did not speak a natural language—he spoke not at all; he grunted and trotted like an animal and bit and scratched those who opposed him.

Itard tells us that his senses "were extraordinarily apathetic. His nostrils were filled with snuff without making him sneeze. He picked up potatoes from boiling water. A pistol fired near him provoked hardly any response though the sound of cracking a walnut caused him to turn round."[21]

Itard tried to teach Victor to speak and read. At the end of 5 years, Victor could identify some written words and phrases referring to objects and actions, and even some words referring to simple relationships such as big and small, and he could use word cards to indicate some of his desires. However, he did not learn to speak; the nature of the small number of written words and phrases he did learn to use remained very much tied to concrete situations.

The story of Victor, whose past history is shrouded in mystery, cannot give us any conclusive evidence as to the fate of children growing up in complete isolation from other humans. There were many people at the time who regarded Victor simply as having been born mentally defective and therefore incapable of acquiring more language than he did, though it would be difficult to explain how a mental defective would be able to fend for himself in the wilds for any length of time.

A more recent case of children growing up in isolation, in this case with wolves, has been described in *Wolf Children and Feral Man,* by I. A. L. Singh and R. M. Zingg, which also contains contributions by several well-known psychologists, including Arnold Gesell.[22] The reports on the discovery of the two children and on their subsequent development was written by an Indian missionary, Singh, who together with his wife cared for the children with utmost devotion. He started writing the diary in the year following the discovery of the children, so the observations concerning the appearance and behavior of the children immediately after their discovery are based on his recollections rather than actual observations; the rest of the diary has many gaps too. He did not, in fact, write the diary for publication, and it was published very much later on the initiative and insistence of the psychologist Zingg, who realized the scientific interest inherent in the case of the two children. Because Singh was a simple man who found it impossible not to mix fact with interpretation, and for other reasons as well, the record is undoubtedly contradictory and unreliable on many details, giving rise to doubts about the genuineness of the whole story. In the most recent edition of the diary (a German translation published in 1964), the Swiss biologist Adolf Portmann has again carefully weighed the evidence and the criticisms, particularly that of Dennis, and has come to the conclusion that, despite the obvious inconsistencies and errors, there is no reason to doubt that in the main the story is true. We shall proceed on this assumption.[23]

In 1920, as the story goes, the Rev. Singh saw a mother wolf and cubs, two of which had long, matted hair and looked human. After considerable preparations and difficulties, the two human creatures were captured. They turned out to be two girls whose ages were assessed by Singh at about 8 years and 1½ years. Singh describes them as "wolfish" in appearance and behavior: They walked on all fours and had calluses on their knees and palms from doing so. They prowled and howled at night; for a long time they remained fond of raw meat and stole it when occasion offered; they slept rolled up in a bundle on the floor; they resisted the approaches of human beings; and they did not speak. With regard to the development of the senses, it was noted that their hearing was very acute and that they could smell meat at a great distance; furthermore, they could orient themselves very well at night. Amala, the younger, died within a year, but Kamala lived until 1929.

By means of intimate and devoted contact with Kamala, by softening her skin with oil and massaging her, by feeding and caressing her, Mrs. Singh was able to win her confidence and to create the conditions in which Kamala would be willing to learn from her. We find, however, that for a long time Kamala preferred the company of cats and dogs to that of children; in the end she came to enjoy children more and more, though her relationship with them, judging by the examples given in the diary, never became easy and secure.

She needed considerable training to stand erect, and we are told that 20 months after having been found she stood erect for the first time. She did not, however, learn to walk on two legs.[24]

As far as language development is concerned, her first recorded attempt at imitating a word spoken by people around her came 2 years and 2 months after she had been rescued. After 6 years of living with human beings, she had a vocabulary of 36 to 40 words, and we are informed that from then on she learned quite a few words and phrases, and even started to speak in sentences. From the examples quoted and the incidents described, one gets the clear impression that despite this progress her language remained very rudimentary and was confined to the concrete and to immediate situations.

No reliable estimate as to the age at which the two children started living with the wolves was possible; their ages at the time of their rescue were mere guesswork on the part of Singh. On evidence from a number of sources, and because it is difficult to imagine a human baby in its first year of life being successfully reared by a wolf, Portmann inclines to the view (also expressed by Dennis) that adoption by the wolf mother could not have been at an age much lower than 2 years. This would mean that the case of Kamala can tell us nothing about the effects of growing up in isolation from human beings, but together with animals, *from birth*. By the age of 2 years, the normal child has been exposed to many humanizing influences, including walking erect and communication by means of language.

If we are correct in assuming that Kamala was at least 2 years old when she joined the wolf family (she might have been older), this would indicate that the first two years of living in a human environment are not sufficient for consolidating the emergence of the characteristically species-bound potentialities of children. This conclusion would also throw a different light on the often-expressed view that children reared in isolation from human beings, or with minimal and perfunctory contact with people, who do not subsequently develop language and continue to lag in intellectual ability were probably born as mental defectives or at least with very poor genetic endowment. It would lend support to the other view—that the development of human intelligence requires continued and close interaction with other people and with the world of human meaning as a necessity, and that where this interaction is missing, the most favorable genetic endowment will be of little avail. A "cultural" variety of feeblemindedness is a well-recognized category in the diagnosis of mental deficiency today.[25]

SOCIAL DEPRIVATION

We can now turn to two cases of a different kind of isolation, in which the children grew up not with animals but in a state of severely reduced contact with human beings. The two girls, Anna and Isabella, are described in various papers by Kingsley Davis, F. N. Maxfield, and Marie C. Mason.[26] Both were born in 1932.

Anna was the second illegitimate child of a farm woman then aged 27 years. For the first 6 to 10 months of her life, the child was shifted from one person and place to another because her maternal grandfather refused to have the baby in the house, where Anna's mother, who worked on his farm, also lived. To those who saw her, including a nurse with whom she boarded for a while, Anna seemed perfectly normal at this stage. She was then taken home to live with her mother at Anna's grandfather's farm, but the grandfather was still so infuriated that he did not wish to see the child. Anna was then confined to one room, where the mother and the older brother also slept. Here she was kept in a chair, half sitting, half reclining most of the time, until she was nearly 6 years old, when she was discovered by the welfare authorities and placed in an institution. Her diet while in the room at home consisted entirely of milk; oatmeal was introduced after her fifth birthday.

Of the attitude of the mother toward her child Davis says: "The mother, resenting the trouble which Anna's presence caused her and wanting to get rid of the girl, paid little attention to her. She apparently did nothing to feed the child, not taking the trouble to bathe, train, supervise, or caress her." Anna's brother, we are told, "seems to have ignored her except to mistreat her occasionally."[27] This is a case, then, not of total isolation from human beings but of "extreme social isolation," as Davis puts it, or, as we might say, of almost total human and educational neglect; the child was kept alive physically, and that was virtually all that was done for her.

When Anna arrived at the institution, she was at first believed to be deaf and dumb. However, careful testing revealed that she turned her head slowly toward a ticking clock placed near her, though she did not respond to hand clapping or speech directed toward her. Her eyes surveyed the room and the ceiling, although it was not clear whether she ever focused on any object. During the testing she remained expressionless, neither smiling nor crying, although she frowned and scowled occasionally "in response to no observable stimulus." Toys presented to her by well-wishers elicited no response, nor did she play. On a performance test of intelligence, she failed completely to register a score. When after about 4 months at the institution, an attempt was made to assess her language development, or rather prelanguage development leading to language, her development was assessed at well below the level of a normal 1-year-old child.

Anna stayed in the institution for 9 months. During this period she was well cared for physically. However, at this institution her interaction with other human beings was also minimal, so in fact her social isolation, though perhaps less harsh, was still extreme. We quote a description of the conditions because we shall have to refer to them again later: "At the latter institution she was early deprived of her two roommates and left alone. In the entire establishment there was only one nurse, who had three hundred and twenty-four other inmates to look after. Most of Anna's care was turned over to adult inmates many of whom were mentally deficient and scarcely able to speak themselves. Part of the time Anna's door was shut. In addition to this continued isolation, Anna was given no stimulus to learning. She was fed, clothed, and cleaned without having to turn a hand on her own behalf. She was never disciplined or rewarded, because nobody had the time for the tedious task. All benefits were for her in the nature of things and therefore not rewards."[28]

At the end of these 9 months, there were a number of improvements in Anna, such as greater alertness, increased ability to fix her attention, a healthier look, and willingness to smile. However, she could still barely stand when holding onto something, and there were still no signs of language development.

She was then removed from the institution and placed in a foster home under the care of a woman who devoted a great deal of attention to her such as is normally given by a mother to her infant. One month after this placement, Davis already noticed "a remarkable transformation," although grave limitations remained. Even after 9 months in the foster home, Anna's language development had only reached the stage where she showed understanding of a number of verbal instructions without being able to speak herself. She lived for 3 more years and at the time of her death had made more progress, but she never achieved anything remotely near normality for a child of her age.

The case of Isabelle, another child who grew up in extraordinary circumstances, is interesting in that it affords some striking parallels to that of Anna and also very striking contrasts. Isabelle was discovered about 9 months after Anna was. She was about the same age at discovery—6½ years old. She too was an illegitimate child and was kept in seclusion for this reason. Here the parallels end. Her mother had developed normally up to the age of 2 years and then, as a result of an accident, had become deaf-mute and had not been educated. From the time the child was born until she was over 6 years of age, mother and child spent their time together in a dark room with the blinds drawn, separated from the rest of the family. The parents of the mother did not permit her to leave the house alone. She eventually escaped, however, carrying her child with her, and in this way Isabelle's case was brought to the notice of the authorities.

As a result of lack of sunlight, fresh air, and proper nutrition, Isabelle had developed a rachitic condition that made locomotion virtually impossible so that she moved about "with a skittering gait." This condition yielded to proper treatment, including surgery, and Isabelle learned to walk and move normally. When her intelligence was first tested via the Stanford-Binet scale at the age of 6½ years, her mental age appeared to be about 19 months. All items involving language were, of course, failed. In the place of normal speech, she made a croaking sound. Though at the very beginning she did not pay attention to the speech of others, it was soon clearly established that in contrast to her mother, who had only minute remnants of hearing in one ear, Isabelle was not deaf.

Isabelle, unlike Anna, was given expert speech training: and she received a great deal of personal attention commencing a few days after her discovery. After a short while her progress in speech became rapid. After less than 2 years, Mason reports, "of changed environment, enriched experiences, unremitting instruction, improved physical condition and appearance (Isabelle) is, at 8 years, considered a child of normal intelligence."[29] Moreover, her relations with other children are described as altogether normal. Her language development had been rapid: She now had a vocabulary of 1500 to 2000 words; she was asking many questions that showed genuine curiosity about things; she could tell a story and make one up; and she enjoyed nursery rhymes and a puppet show, which indicates that she could now create and share with others a world of imagination and was not confined in her use of language to the immediate and the concrete.

Mason and Davis regard this case as proof of what a properly conceived and directed process of speech training can achieve even after 6 years of extreme social isolation. Undoubtedly they are right in attributing an extremely important role to the approach used, and in any case of failure to "rehabilitate" a child that has grown up in isolation, relative or complete, it may well be that the program of care and of training and education has been hopelessly at fault. It may be that the Wild Boy of Aveyron, who certainly received a great deal of devoted attention from Itard, received the wrong sort of attention. Possibly Itard's methods of language training were based on wrong notions concerning the nature of language and language development—though a noted modern psycholinguist, Roger Brown, says at the beginning of his book *Words and Things*, published in 1958: "The doctor's [i.e., Itard's] methods of instruction were founded on an analysis of the basic psychology of language which is the same as the analysis on which the present book is founded."[30] The failure to train Kamala to speak may be due to the insufficiency of the methods used by the devoted, but scientifically untrained, Singh couple. The psychological and educational neglect of Anna for the first 9 months after her discovery and the lack of expert care thereafter may account for much of Anna's poor showing. There is, however, another aspect of all the different cases described that had not received the attention which in my belief it deserves.

Although both Anna and Isabelle grew up in dark rooms, isolated from the rest of the family, we cannot simply equate the psychological meaning of the conditions under which they grew up. In view of the fact that Isabelle's mother was quite incapable of speaking, it may seem as though Isabelle suffered a deprivation and neglect even greater than that of Anna. However, the psychological relationship between mother and child seems to have been very different in the two cases. Anna's mother completely rejected her child: "The mother, resenting the trouble which Anna's presence caused her and *wanting to get rid of the child*" (italics added), spent as little time as possible with her. The brother ignored or mistreated his sister. She knew, from birth onward, only a hostile world, with possibly a few exceptions during short spells in the first months of her life. The fact that her mother could speak did not mean that she did speak to Anna or that she ever gave Anna the feeling of being an individual—an individual who was loved and valued and important, and nothing the child may have done spontaneously was encouraged or supported by the interest and closeness of any other person.

When we look at the mother-child relationship in the case of Isabelle, we find a very different situation. However pathetic the relationship may have been, Isabelle's mother was *with her child* all the time. The fact that when the situation became unbearable for Isabelle's mother she *escaped with her child*, not attempting in her desperation to forsake her, suggests that there must have been a strong bond between mother and child.

Marie Mason gives an account of her first contact with Isabelle, which ocurred after the child had been in the hospital for only a few days, during which time she had been in tears continuously. The striking point in this account is that Isabelle is able to relate to a person relatively easily. According to Bowlby, Spitz, and others who have studied the effects of "maternal deprivation,"[31] such relating is not possible for children who have not had contact with a person who loves them and whom they can trust. Isabelle seems to have had such an experience with her mother, despite the fact the rest of the world rejected both her and her mother.

Moreover, she had *communicated* with her mother, because the mother communicated with her. It is a mistake for one to assume that all communication between human beings is dependent on spoken language. There is nonverbal communication of feeling and intention, which proceeds via physical contact and bodily expression and pantomime and gestures. In deaf-mutes this form of communication is often highly developed. Nonverbal communication is extremely limited, it is true, and in the absence of exposure to the spoken language of human beings, it alone cannot lead to the development of speech.[32] But it implies a human relatedness, a communion between at least two persons, and a desire to communicate with someone. These are some of the indispensible prerequisites to the development of speech, even in a child that grows up under normal circumstances.

The earliest record of the contact between the speech specialist and Isabelle, which occurred a few days after her entry to the hospital (recall that Isabelle was then 6½ years old), shows not only the human relatedness but also Isabelle's use of gestures:

Sensing that any direct approach which I might take would not only be of no avail but might disastrously affect any future confidence, I pretended absorption in a doll brought to me by Jane, another child in the same ward. Covertly watching Isabelle, I chose a chair close to her and drew Jane and the doll to my lap. I glanced up casually to find Isabelle watching me. I gave her a friendly smile but made no attempt to engage her attention. Soon her attitude of repulsion gave way to one of curiosity. *She made a gesture with the palm of her hand first raised to me and then to the child in my lap* [italics added]. This I interpreted as her desire to discover the relationship between Jane and myself. I felt that she wanted to know whether the child belonged to me.[33]

A child who makes that kind of gesture, who makes contact with a person so relatively easily, and who shows curiosity about the relationship of a strange child to a strange woman must surely have experienced a basic relatedness to her mother herself (an experience denied to a girl like Anna) and must have communicated with her mother in gestures, too. Although the record contains very few references to this aspect of her early experience, we also get a glimpse of it from this statement:

Gesture was her only mode of expression. In her characteristic descriptive motions with which she tried to make clear what she wanted, I noted *a similarity to the sign language used by deaf children* . . . [italics added]. These observations prompted me, therefore, to adopt an educational approach combining gesture, facial expression, pantomime, dramatization and imitation.[34]

In his paper on Isabelle published in 1947, 7 years after the publication of his paper on Anna, Davis inclines to the view that, perhaps despite his earlier view, Anna (in contrast to Isabelle) had been born feebleminded. This is a possibility one can never rule out. However, it seems to me that Davis overlooked the psychological meaning of the basic mother-child relationship, since he seemed simply to equate the two cases of "extreme social isolation," with the odds apparently against Isabelle because of her deaf-mute mother. Nor can one simply equate the cases of Anna and Isabelle with those of Amala and Kamala, the feral girls. A girl like Anna had formed no relationship with any being, either human or animal. Amala and Kamala had formed such relationships to animals during a period when the plasticity and "openness" of the child is still at its highest; thus, upon returning to human society, they had to unlearn something that in its way was a positive mode of life too. Isabelle alone had been in close contact and interaction with her human, though immensely handicapped and speechless, mother, who nevertheless accepted her. Whatever we may surmise about the genetic endowment of the four children, it is only Isabelle who had the advantage of close contact with her mother. This gave her the basic experiences of being valued and of being communicated with, and after her rescue she had both untutored and expert human care and education. Thus, it was only Isabelle who was able in the end to lead a meaningful life in a human society. While we are still left with an unknown factor—the genetic endowment of each of these children—it seems highly unlikely that Anna would not have shown far greater advances in the direction of humanization if she had enjoyed the advantages given Isabelle in her early life and after her mother removed her from isolation.

THE EDUCATIONAL DIMENSION

We have just referred to the differences the mother-child relationship, communication, and specific training and education make in developing the forms of behavior characteristic of the human species: walking erect and speech. This brings us to consideration of the specifically educational aspect implied in Langeveld's conception of the child as *animal educandum* and in Montagu's statement that "being human is not a status with which but to which one is born."

The young of other species do not start life fully grown; the ape, for instance, also has to learn the behavior of his species and adapt himself to the requirements of living in his group by growing up in his group. And an ape in captivity does not behave in all respects like an ape roaming about freely in nature with his group. However, the human infant is much more helpless than the young of any other species, and the period of helplessness lasts very much longer. Apart from this, there is much more involved in human growing up than just being "socialized" and acquiring the ways of the group through interaction with others.

From the point of view of equipment with formed patterns of behavior that are ready to function and will enable him to survive— that is, reflexes and instincts—the human infant is an unimpressive creature. He is at first completely, and for many years partially, dependent on the ministrations of others if he is even to survive, let alone grow vigorously. This "biological deficit" with which the human infant is born makes him initially vulnerable, but it is also the condition that makes it necessary and possible for those in whose care he is to influence and mold him, and to provide opportunities for him to develop in ways considered appropriate.

As we have already seen, a child needs a certain minimum of human interaction and care in order to develop, in at least some minimal way, what we regard as the distinguishing characteristics of his species. But this minimal human interaction is not enough to develop in the child his full potentialities as an individual *person.* The newborn child is experienced by the mother and the father not as a biological representative of the species *Homo sapiens* but as "our child," born into our particular family at a particular point in time and thus dependent on us for a long time to come. Into their spontaneous care for the child, there enters almost imperceptibly the specific *educational* concern for the child: the desire to let the child become a certain kind of person. Some spontaneous tendencies of the child are encouraged, others are checked, forbidden, or simply eliminated by paying no attention to them. It is not simply by interacting with the child but by the specific educational intent of many of the adult's actions in relation to the child that the child's potentialities as an individual person are actualized.

As an individual person the child grows up in a particular family, society, civilization, and culture, and like his educators he is subject to all the possibilities and limitations inherent in these groups. It is not sufficient, however, to say simply that the child is "conditioned" by his culture or that what he will become depends entirely on his culture. However much the educator (parent or teacher), in educating the child and helping him become a mature adult who will be capable of taking responsibility for his own actions and leading his own meaningful life as an individual person, may follow customs and conventions (how unbearably complicated life would be without customs and conventions to relieve us of at least some of our decisions!), the educator must continually make choices. These choices are made in the light of the educator's image of the kind of personal life that is worth living, both for himself and for this particular child. He tries to educate the child according to these ideas and images.

The child, however, is not merely a conditionable organism. By this we mean he is not merely some object to be conditioned or trained, despite the plasticity that is the hallmark of human beings in general. There are limits to what we can "make" out of an individual child. Rather, we mean that the child does not merely react to what adults try to do to him—that is, to their actions that are intended to educate. On the contrary, the child himself is active in giving meaning to his gradually expanding world; he too is an accepting and rejecting human being. At least where the circumstances are not too strongly against the child (as in extreme neglect and isolation or, at the other extreme, when the image of the adult, by which he tries to help and educate the child, is altogether unrealistic for this particular child), the child shows a strong urge to make his own contribution to the shaping of his own world and person.

It is in the basic human situation of relatedness of an adult (parent or surrogate) to a helpless child that regulation of behavior with educational intent becomes one of the components of the adult-child relationship. The specifically educational concern for the child has its natural point of entry here, but it points to a realm other than biological inevitability. It points to the realm of society and culture, which man has created and in regard to which he is on the one hand bound and limited by what already exists and on the other free, as well as required, to make choices. Such choices are not only of means toward ends established by nature but also of what is desirable and valuable, worthy of human existence.

When we consider child development in the context of education (and child development never occurs without education except in "extreme social isolation," which no society condones), then what a child *should* become cannot be separated from the question of what he *is*: He is a being in the process of becoming, and education carries the *should* into this process. This makes possible his development, not simply as a representative of a biological species but concretely as an individual person subject to historical time, place, and circumstance. The child is *animal educandum*, the animal that must be educated, because man is a being forever in search of himself. He is faced with the necessity of choosing, subject to limiting conditions and in the face of countless possibilities, what he will become.

It is necessary now to follow up some of the implications of this statement. Chapter 3, "A Child's Basic Psychological Needs," will expand on the helplessness of the child and relate this to his educational development. In Chapter 4, "Man as *Animal Symbolicum*," we shall turn to language again, this time in order to elucidate an important aspect of man's relationship to his culture and to see some implications for our understanding of what is involved for the child in assimilating his culture.

Topics for
Further Exploration

1. "Some spontaneous tendencies of the child are encouraged [by the parent], others are checked, forbidden or simply eliminated by paying no attention to them." Observe some parent-child interactions and read Joseph Church's *Three Babies: Biographies of Cognitive Development* (New York: Random House, 1966) with a view to answering the questions: Could it be that some spontaneous tendencies or exhibited behaviors of the child are not even seen by the parent, while others that barely show are seen and responded to eagerly? What are the implications of this for the development of the child?

2. Adult expectations with regard to abilities and scholastic attainments of children have been studied experimentally. Read Rosenthal and Jacobson, *Pygmalion in the Classroom* (New York: Holt, Rinehart & Winston, 1968); then formulate your conclusions on the following educational issues: (a) In what ways, verbal and nonverbal, does the teacher in the classroom convey his expectations to individual children? (b) What effects is the practice of grouping classes in school according to level of intelligence and past scholastic attainment likely to have on the level of aspiration and self-image of the children?

3. Toward the end of the chapter, we pointed to two factors in determining the direction of development in the child: (a) parental (and other adult) expectations and (b) the child's autonomy. It is obvious that the two may be in conflict; this conflict is often resolved, if at all, only in adolescence and adulthood. Trace in your own life the parental (and other adults') expectations that have given direction to your interests, abilities, and choice of career, and the assertion of your own autonomy in shaping your own life. Then, in order to gain perspective on the forces at work, read Robert W. White, *Lives in Progress: A Study of the Natural Growth of Personality* (New York: Holt, Rinehart & Winston, 1957), particularly the three autobiographies.

References and Comments

1.   M. F. Ashley Montagu, *The Direction of Human Development* (London: Watts, 1955), p. 85.

2. M. J. Langeveld, *Studien zur Anthropologie des Kindes* (Tübingen: Max Niemeyer Verlag, 3d enl. ed., 1968; 1st ed., 1956).

3. The terms *anthropology of the child* or, more frequently, *anthropology of education* are more likely to occur in publications in German, such as Werner Loch, *Die anthropologische Dimension der Pädagogik* (Essen: Deutsche Schule Verlagsgesellschaft, 1963) and Herbert Becker, ed., *Anthropologie und Pädagogik* (Bad Heilbronn, 1967). However, they occur in English publications too.

   It is not the term that matters but the issues that are raised; William Kessen's *The Child* (New York: Wiley, 1966), containing historical readings that illustrate different conceptions of what a child is, deals with the anthropology of the child. The practical importance of dealing with different conceptions of the child is evident: The explicit and implicit assumptions about childhood and the child influence our rearing and educating of children.

   Ashley Montagu's book *The Direction of Human Development*, op. cit., also deals with the anthropology of the child; though he examines a great deal of what is known from research about the origins of aggressiveness, cooperativeness, and love in children, he goes far beyond empirical facts and tries to look at their meaning in terms of the total process of development and a viable conception of man.

4. M. Landmann, *Philosophische Anthropologie* (Berlin: Sammlung Göschen, Walter de Gruyter, 1955).

5. Contrast Margaret Mead's descriptions in *Coming of Age in Samoa* and *Growing Up in New Guinea*, both available in Penguin Books; originally published in 1928 and 1930, respectively.

6. R. R. Sears, Eleanor Maccoby, and H. Levin, *Patterns of Child Rearing* (New York: Harper & Row, 1957).

   J. W. M. Whiting and I. L. Child, *Child Training and Personality* (New Haven: Yale University Press, 1953).

7. The best-known example is that reported by Mary D. Salter Ainsworth in *Infancy in Uganda* (Baltimore: Johns Hopkins Press, 1967), chap. 19, and by Marcelle Geber, referred to by Ainsworth. Similar findings come from other parts of Africa; see, e.g., K. Theunnissen, "A Preliminary Comparative Study of the Development of Motor Behavior in European and Bantu Children Up to the Age of One Year" (M.A. thesis, University of South Africa, 1948).

8. See M. F. Ashley Montagu, *The Biosocial Nature of Man* (New York: Grove, 1956) for a discussion of Freud's view of man.

9. Ashley Montagu, *The Direction of Human Development*, op. cit.

10. E.g., M. F. Ashley Montagu, *On Being Human* (New York: Abelard-Schuman, 1950); *Helping Children Develop Moral Values* (Chicago: Science Research, 1953).

11. Ashley Montagu, *On Being Human*, ibid.

12. W. Köhler, *The Mentality of Apes* (Baltimore: Pelican; first published in 1917).

   R. M. Yerkes, *Chimpanzees* (New Haven: Yale University Press, 1943).

   W. N. and L. A. Kellogg, *The Ape and the Child* (New York: McGraw-Hill, 1933).

13. Ashley Montagu, *On Being Human*, op. cit.

14. Cathy Hayes, *The Ape in Our House* (New York: Harper & Row, 1951).

15. Cathy Hayes, ibid., particularly chap. 21, "Over the Fence and Off to Mrs. Clarke's."

16. R. A. Gardner and Beatrice T. Gardner, "Teaching Sign Language to a Chimpanzee," *Science* 165 (1969):664–672.

17. D. McNeill, *The Acquisition of Language* (New York: Harper & Row, 1970).

18. D. Premack, "The Education of Sarah," *Psychology Today* 4, 4 (1970):54–58.

19. R. A. Chase, "Evolutionary Aspects of Language Development and Function," in F. Smith and G. A. Miller eds., *The Genesis of Language*, eds. F. Smith and G. A. Miller (Cambridge: M.I.T. Press, 1966).

20. J. M. G. Itard, *The Wild Boy of Aveyron*, trans. with intro. by George Humphrey (New York: Appleton, 1932).

21. Itard, quoted in Kingsley Davis, "Extreme Social Isolation of a Child," *American Journal of Sociology* 45 (1940):563.

22. J. A. L. Singh and R. M. Zingg, *Wolf Children and Feral Man, Contributions to the University of Denver* (New York and London: 1942).

23. J. A. L. Singh, *Die "Wolfskinder" von Midnapore, mit einem Geleitwort von Adolf Portmann* (The wolf children of Midnapore, with commentary by Adolf Portmann) (Heidelberg: Quelle und Meyer, 1964). For the criticism by Dennis, see W. Dennis, "The Significance of Feral Man," *American Journal of Psychology* 54 (1941):425–432, and for a further analysis of reports of wolf children, see *Child Development* 22 (1951):153–158.

24. Roger Brown, in *Words and Things* (Glencoe, Ill.: Free Press, 1958), p. 190, says: "In time Kamala learned to walk erect, . . ." I cannot find any evidence for this either in the diary as published by Singh and Zingg or in the German translation of Portmann. She seems to have learned to *stand* erect, but not to walk on two legs.
25. See, e.g., R. L. Masland et al., *Mental Subnormality* (New York: Basic Books, 1958).
26. Kingsley Davis, "Extreme Social Isolation of a Child," *American Journal of Sociology* 45 (1940):554–565. Also, see Kingsley Davis, "Final Note on a Case of Extreme Isolation," *American Journal of Sociology* 52 (1947): 432–437.

    Marie K. Mason, "Learning to Speak After Six and One-Half Years of Silence," *Journal of Speech and Hearing Disorders* 7 (1942): 295–304.
27. See *American Journal of Sociology* 45 (1940):557.
28. Ibid., p. 560.
29. See *Journal of Speech and Hearing Disorders* 7 (1942):304.
30. Brown, op. cit., p. 4.
31. John Bowlby, *Child Care and the Growth of Love* (Calif.: Pelican, first published in 1953). This book is based on a report written for the World Health Organization.

    John Bowlby, *Maternal Care and Mental Health* (Geneva: World Health Organization, Monograph Series no. 2, 1951).

    See also World Health Organization, Geneva, *Deprivation of Maternal Care. A Reassessment of Its Effects* (Public Health Papers no. 14, 1962).
32. See also Chapter 4.
33. *Journal of Speech and Hearing Disorders* 7 (1942):296.
34. Ibid., p. 299.

CHAPTER 3

A Child's Basic Psychological Needs

From birth on, therefore, each infant is engaged in creating a highly selective environment or a "life space" that is as congenial and appropriate for his individualized organism, with its peculiar needs and capacities, as is possible under the constraints and coercions imposed by others upon his growth, development, functioning, and learning.[1]

    Lawrence K. Frank

Toward the end of Chapter 2 we said a child needs a certain minimum of human interaction and care in order to develop the distinguishing biological characteristics of his species in at least a minimal way but that this minimal human interaction is not enough to develop the full potentialities of the child as an individual person. The child is dependent on others, especially in infancy. Leaving the child simply to grow up among people, but with no specific person or persons devoting themselves to him and taking responsibility for the direction his development is to take, would leave to chance such direction and the subsequent development of the child's potentialities as a person. Of course, chance (that is, the numerous unpredictable contingencies of life) will always play a role; different "environments" offer different possibilities to children and, thus, different possibilities to parents and educators in educating them. But in whatever environment and culture a child grows up, no society condones educational neglect of the child. The child everywhere is not just a child; he is also an educand, with a special relationship to those who educate him. The educand-educator relationship is a basic human relationship, but it is of a special kind. Its distinctive feature is that one person, the educator (mother, father, teacher, priest, uncles and aunts, etc.) is more mature and acts for and on behalf of, and in the immediate as well as long-term interests of the educand, who is less mature and in no position to know what is "necessary" and what is "possible." The educator-educand relationship is also a cooperative situation in which the educator cannot impose just *any* direction and pattern of development on the child regardless of the nature of the particular child and of the child's impulses, intentions, and aspirations.

REFLECTIVENESS AND NONREFLECTIVENESS IN EDUCATION

In some societies and in some families, what the educator does in educating the child may be at a predominantly nonreflective level, where everything is determined by conventions and mores. In Margaret Mead's studies of children growing up in New Guinea and Samoa[2] we have examples of such societies; descriptions of child-rearing practices in various parts of Europe[3] show the same kind of reliance on time-hallowed assumptions about what ought to be done in the upbringing and education of children at different age levels.

Such predominantly nonreflective care for and education of children is characteristic of social groups in which adulthood is defined by a narrow range of possibilities so that anything that falls outside those possibilities can be disregarded. Thus, child rearing and education can be geared to the relatively few roles the children will later have to play in adult society, generation after generation. It is easy to see that when the handling of the child is at the predominantly nonreflective level, with few doubts and uncertainties arising in the educators, the child is likely to feel secure. But it is obvious also that under these circumstances innumerable possibilities of human development are likely to remain dormant, although the child himself, as well as the unreflecting educators, will not be aware of this failure to maximize his potential.

The situation in Western society today is very different. Although a great deal of child care and education is still guided by custom, we have become much more self-conscious about the relationships between child care and education on the one hand and the development of personality and the potentialities of the individual on the other. As a result, custom is no longer rooted in the practice of many generations but more typically in that of only the previous generation, if that: Mothers study the newest published guides to the upbringing of babies and preschool children but rely on what their own mothers did—or on what their mothers *tell* them they did. Because of this, the practices of the school are usually those of the previous generation of school teachers, but they are also (it is hoped) modified in the light of newer ideas.[4]

People are uncertain of how to bring up children and educate them, not simply because they have become more reflective through education of a formal kind but also as a result of their faith in what "science," or psychology, teaches. A need for more reflectiveness in the upbringing and education of children has arisen because preparation for adulthood today is so much more complex than it used to be and because we have accepted the notion that there are numerous potentialities in children that are only realized through proper care and education.

CULTURE AND PERSONALITY

Our civilization is seen more and more to depend not only on preparing individuals to play predestined and roughly definable roles in a static society but also on developing creative individuals who can cope with change in the conditions of living. Such people may also bring about changes that will increase still further the opportunities open to future generations and, in doing so, enrich other lives as well as their own.

The enormous amount of energy devoted to studying the relationship between culture and personality, and, more specifically, early childhood practices and adult personality[5] did not yield decisive results, mainly because psychologists were too often looking for a complete determinism, whereas culture or early childhood practices should be regarded only as codeterminers of behavior or cognitive development or personality development. Through its socialization practices and through sheer exposure of the child to the dominant values, customs, and habits of a particular culture, the frame of reference for the child's development is created. But different children, in interaction with various educators, will respond differently, and the long-term effects of such interaction may turn out to vary widely.[6] There can be no question of a strict determinism; this is also borne out by some of the more recent research on the early development of creative individuals. It is significant that in the research on creativity, interest has shifted to finding conditions that *encourage* or make *possible* the emergence of creativity in the growing person[7] without being able to guarantee it.

PSYCHOLOGICAL NEEDS

Among the conditions that will profoundly affect the child's development as a person and the realization of his potentialities are those that relate to the child's basic psychological needs. There is a curious ambiguity about the meaning of the word "needs." The dictionary lists its meaning as "that which is wanted," but it is also defined as "requirement." We may want—even crave—things that do us harm in the long run. What we require in the long term we may not particularly want at the moment. Not all wants, wishes, and momentary whims are needs in the sense of being "requirements." And what a requirement is in the development of a child must always be seen in relation to some condition or end-state that is regarded as "desirable" or "essential," but in any case as being in the interest of the child. Defining something as a basic psychological need of the child always involves *relating a child's momentary behavior and condition to its implications for a shorter or a longer stretch of the child's development and deciding what is "desirable" or even "essential" to the development of this particular child.*

There is a further point that should be stressed. People generally, and children in particular, may *feel* a need without being able to formulate it in words. Also, as Freud has taught us, thwarted and repressed needs express themselves in behavior, often devious behavior seemingly unrelated to any kind of rational purpose. The infant or child who cannot tell us in words what it is that he is in need of nevertheless has needs that must be met if he is to develop healthily, and he is dependent on adults to interpret those needs correctly. The adult does this by being responsive to the behavioral and nonverbal cues that emanate from the child. There is a great deal of interpretation involved here, and what one adult may regard as a need may not be seen as such by another.

MASLOW'S NEEDS

We have been saying that basic psychological needs must be seen in the context of the basic educational relationship within which the development of a child takes place. We stress this point because we want to present an alternative to the view that needs are "instinctual" (Freud) or "instinctoid" (Maslow) tendencies, which can only be *either* gratified (directly or in sublimated form) *or* frustrated and repressed. What we shall argue instead is that how the educator helps the child cope with his felt needs and what he does to make the child become aware of (to feel) *new needs* and to help him cope with these is crucial to the development of the potentialities of the child and of his personality.

Maslow has presented a theory of basic needs that is perhaps the best known in the Anglo-American world today and, although it was developed from experience in psychotherapy with adults, has considerable relevance for a theory of basic needs that tries to focus on the basic educational relationship in child development.[8] We shall describe this theory and reinterpret it in line with our special focus on the educational relationship involved. As will become evident, his theory has serious weaknesses, but it is challenging and enables us to examine the concept of needs.

In one important respect Maslow's theory is entirely concordant with arguments we have been expounding; he relates the satisfaction or thwarting of the basic needs of the child to the basic question: What kind of adult personality do we want to see developing? His theory differs from most theories concerning basic needs in that the latter usually *imply*, rather than explicitly state, certain conceptions of what constitutes desirable personality development. The other theories simply take for granted that everyone shares a common conception of human nature.[9] Just as we say "the body needs food" without specifying the criteria by which this becomes a valid statement, so more complex basic psychological needs are often posited without clearly formulated criteria by which we can judge statements about them. Most of us are so culture- and *Zeitgeist*-bound that what constitutes desirable personality development seems obvious. But of course it is not at all obvious. What is self-evident to us may not be to people living in a very different culture or in a very different time. Among the Kpelle in Liberia, Gay and Cole tell us, "The child who asks, 'Why?' is considered 'frisky' and is beaten for his curiosity."[10] If a Puritan from the seventeenth century heard people from the twentieth century saying "a child needs to be able to assert itself" or "a child needs to have plenty of opportunity for playing," he would be horrified and retort: "a child needs to be obedient and to have its will broken" or "a child must learn, as early as possible, not to waste time on play, which is an invention of the Devil."[11]

Maslow's criterion is a view of the desirable, mature personality, which is also culture-bound. But this does not mean it simply reflects adult personalities as they are commonly found in North America at present. On the contrary, Maslow's view reflects the present concern throughout the Western world with developing new potentialities in human beings (the stress on creativity) and with developing the potentialities of individuals who in the past have been deprived of opportunity (in culturally deprived and underdeveloped countries). This concern reflects the widely prevalent mood of not accepting the usual as the inevitable, seeing "adaptation as the enemy of adaptability," and emphasizing the creative possibilities in human nature. The fact that this conception is culture-bound does not discredit it; on the contrary, it makes Maslow's theory of basic psychological needs relevant to significant aspirations of people in our age.

How does Maslow arrive at his conception of the mature personality? He asserts that if we are to understand the needs of the child, we must gather our data about personality development not only from so-called "average" people (normal in the statistical sense) but above all from those who, however rare they may be, represent an

ideal of personality development that shows us what such development can lead to. According to Maslow, the average adult, who is
reasonably well adjusted to the demands of society and reasonably
free of "neurotic traits," may be psychologically healthy only in the
sense of being free of incapacitating psychological illness. This
cannot be the goal of human development: "Not sick" does not
equal "well and healthy."

The kind of mature personality Maslow sets up as an example
of "positive mental health" and as a criterion by which one can
identify needs is arrived at by studying a very select sample of
contemporary and historical people who in Maslow's judgment were
really mature. He then tries to formulate what it is about these
people that makes us regard them as truly mature. All this—the selection of the people for study, the judgments about them—involves, of
course, Maslow's own "subjective" evaluation of what is desirable. He
is the first to admit this, but instead of apologizing for it he asserts,
quite rightly, that this is unavoidable and even necessary: We cannot
study human behavior without letting questions of value intrude into
our thinking. The psychologist cannot afford to leave questions of
value, of what ought to be, unformulated; it is better that they be
explicitly stated. In any case, it is concern for the quality of human
life that leads us to look at the possibilities inherent in children and
at their "needs." Whether Maslow is right in his view that the *ought*
can be inferred from the *is* (a completely naturalistic ethic) is a
matter for philosophers to speculate on.

The mature person, as Maslow sees him, is characterized above
all by an ongoing process of "self-actualization," a term he borrows
from Kurt Goldstein.[12] The mature person's behavior is no longer
heavily dependent on what other people do to or for him, or what
they think or feel about him: He has been set free to explore the
world and to discover new potentialities in himself, which he can
then try to define. "Just as the tree needs sunshine and water and
food," says Maslow, "so do most people need love, safety, and the
other basic need gratifications that come only from without. But
once these external need satisfiers are obtained, once these inner
deficiencies are satiated by outside satisfiers, the true *problem of
human development begins*, i.e. self-actualization, . . ." (italics
added).

Maturity, then, involves not being preoccupied with basic needs that can only be satisfied by dependence on other people; it involves being open to the world as it is and discovering in it new meaning, and developing in oneself new potentialities. Among the numerous characteristics of self-actualizing persons that Maslow lists, we find:

1. They have greater personal autonomy, independence, and self-reliance—all of which do not preclude but rather make possible involvement with and care for other people, who are seen not as gratifiers or thwarters of one's own emotional needs but as persons in their own right.
2. They focus on problems outside themselves, and they can become completely absorbed in an activity for its own sake.
3. They are capable even of what Maslow calls "mystic experiences," which he defines as "a tremendous intensification of any of the experiences in which there is a loss of self or transcendence of it, e.g., problem-centering, intense concentration . . . intense sensuous experience, self-forgetful and intense enjoyment of music or art."
4. They accept the unknown, the ambiguous, and the mysterious instead of avoiding and evading it. Maslow quotes Einstein's remark: "The most beautiful thing is the mysterious. It is the source of all art and science."
5. They are superior in the perception of reality; that is, their perception is less distorted by anxiety, prejudice, and the projection of their own wishes.
6. They are more aware of their own impulses, desires, beliefs, and subjective reactions; that is, they really know themselves better than most people do, and they face up to themselves more.
7. They are more spontaneous and creative, not in the sense of exercising a special talent or producing great works but in the sense of being able to see things freshly, transcending accepted and conventionbound ways of seeing things.
8. They feel themselves responsible for the society of which they are members; that is, they see society not only as it is but also as it should and could be.

The self-actualizing person not only continues to discover new potentialities in himself but is also concerned with *becoming* what he can be: "What a man can be, he must be," says Maslow.[13] As he discovers new potentialities, he feels invited or challenged to actualize them.

Let us now take a closer look at the basic needs posited by Maslow and at the relationships between them. He lists six groups of needs, although about aesthetic needs he speaks so tentatively that we shall leave them out of our account. For ease of presentation we shall first give the list in diagrammatic form:

High or less basic	Need for self-actualization
	Need for knowing and understanding
	Need for esteem
	Need for love and feeling of belonging
	Need for safety
Low or most basic	Physiological needs

The distinction between "higher" and "lower" needs implies levels of maturity in the development of the personality. As soon as a higher need has become an actual motivator of behavior, a more mature stage of development has been reached. However, the higher needs do not become actual motivators of behavior unless lower needs have previously functioned as such motivators and have been gratified; hence, the lower needs may be said to be more "basic"—their satisfaction is a necessary *basis* for the emergence of higher needs.

Maslow speaks of a "hierarchy of prepotency" of needs. The lower needs are prepotent over the higher ones, but once they are sufficiently gratified they lose their strength as actual determinants of behavior, and the next-higher need becomes prepotent.

As Maslow sees it, it is only a *felt* need that motivates behavior. We remind ourselves, however, that a felt need is not necessarily synonymous with a need that can be formulated in words by the person experiencing the need. If the need for food—one of the physiological needs—is not satisfied, the craving for food becomes a preoccupation, leaving no room for any other motivation. But:

The physiological needs, along with their partial goals, when chronically gratified cease to exist as active determinants or organizers of behavior. They now exist only in the sense that they may emerge again to dominate the organism if they are thwarted. But a want that is satisfied is no longer a want. The organism is

dominated and its behavior organized only by unsatisfied needs.
If hunger is satisfied, it becomes unimportant in the current
dynamics of the individual.[14]

When a person is freed from the preoccupation with one basic
need, a less basic and higher need begins to assert itself and demands
satisfaction: "If the psychological needs are relatively well gratified,
there then emerges a new set of needs, which we may roughly
categorize as the safety needs." And so on, up the scale toward ever-
higher needs: Unless the need for security is sufficiently met, the
need for love and for a sense of unconditional belonging cannot
become a strong actual motivator of behavior; unless the need for
love is sufficiently gratified and has led to deep and true relationships
to people (at least to the mother), the need for esteem is not
strongly felt; unless all of these needs are adequately met so that
they do not become a preoccupation, the child's natural tendency
to explore and interpret his world and his own experience (need for
knowing and understanding) cannot become strong; and without
being attracted to the world and wanting to know and understand it,
one cannot become aware of one's own potentialities and accept the
challenge of the need for self-actualization.

What Maslow is saying is that strongly felt needs of the child
must be identified and gratified, and that gratification leads to an
ever-widening circle of more mature behavior. But while his whole
book deals with the effects of gratification as against frustration of
needs, he does recognize that gratification is not, as he puts it, the
"only source of strength" for the developing personality: "It is probably true that higher needs may occasionally emerge, not after
gratification, but rather after forced or voluntary deprivation, renunciation, or suppression of lower basic needs and gratifications. . . ."[15]
However, he devotes little space to examining these possibilities
except to say that they should be explored.

EDUCATION AND MASLOW'S NEEDS

From our own focus on the educational relationship within which
child development takes place, it becomes very clear that it is necessary to explore these possibilities. Does the gratification of lower needs

lead necessarily, almost automatically, to the emergence of higher needs? And is the highest need, the need for "self-actualization, the coming to full development and actuality of the potentialities of the organism," really, as Maslow says, "not acquired from without, but . . . rather an unfolding from within of what is, in a subtle sense, already there"? Is the role of the educator merely that of identifying and gratifying, or allowing the child to gratify, needs as they begin to emerge and show themselves in the behavior of the child? Is there really a biologically preordained sequence of emergence of needs leading to self-actualization of the potentialities of the "organism," provided only the child's needs at each stage are gratified?

Seen in an educational context, the emergence of new, more mature needs in the child does not follow automatically from having his needs gratified. The adult must help the child *cope* with needs, which involves not only gratification but also renunciation and assigning priorities. The situation must be deliberately structured in such a way that new needs will arise and be felt, and their challenge will be met. And the child must be helped to develop a pattern of accepted needs, which enables him to develop a particular qualitative variation of the human mature person.

A need points to a *lack*. The need for food arises from a lack, which can only be removed by a sufficient and appropriate supply of food. Therefore, the first question we always have to ask in connection with the needs of a child is: Is there a sufficient *supply* of whatever it is that is lacking? Referring specifically to the needs posited by Maslow, we would mean food and the right kind of food; relevant conditions in the immediate environment that make for security; willingness and ability of the adults involved to give love and to accept the child unconditionally; opportunity for the infant and the child to prove his own powers to himself and willingness on the part of the people around him, particularly his educators, to value the child for what he is accomplishing; an environment in which the child can explore; intellectual stimulation, including particularly linguistic interaction with parents; and an environment in which the actualization of potentialities is valued and encouraged.

Moreover, a need manifests itself in the child as a *felt* need. But when a need is felt, there may be no clear awareness of the "object" capable of gratifying the need. This point is very important to the parent and the educator generally: Needs do not all express themselves as clearly and unmistakably as the need for food, and not all impulses, tendencies, and desires reflect needs that *must* be met. Moreover, needs that manifest themselves in the behavior of the child only as the merest indications or possibilities (e.g., in the questions a child of 3 or 4 years is asking about things he has observed) may in fact be very significant from a point of view of long-term personality development.[16] New needs emerge, in fact, not only as a result of the gratification of previous, more basic, needs but also as a result of the child's interactions with his world (transactional process) and as a result of experience; the educational task may be not so much to gratify already manifest needs as to help the child develop new needs (whether or not previous needs have been fully gratified) and to strengthen these as *felt* needs. Would a child feel a need to study systematically physics, chemistry, and biology at school if we did not structure the situation in such a way that the need arises and is felt? Would mere curiosity be enough?

Finally, the infant, the growing child, or even the adolescent cannot satisfy his own needs unaided. The newborn infant has a need for food as well as a need to be fed. From the beginning there is a cooperative situation. The mother not only provides and offers the supply of milk; she also *supports* the baby's own efforts to feed itself. This may be taken as prototypical of all needs, whether we think of the bodily ones such as the need for food or elimination of body wastes, or of those that arise from the human being's directedness toward a world outside himself and his attempts to relate himself meaningfully to it. The emphasis, of course, shifts to increasing self-reliance in coping with needs, but with each new need that arises the dependence on support from the educator becomes evident again, until finally the child is an adult who will have to rely on his own ability to cope with his needs.

THE PATTERN OF NEEDS

As a formal pattern to guide us in our thinking, we can therefore establish the following:

1. Each child has *needs* (lacks), and some of these are strongly felt needs that motivate his behavior; others arise as a result of experience and confrontation with new situations and tasks that the educator sets. The school in particular confronts the child with new situations and tasks that can make him aware of entirely new needs: the need to acquire the culturally evolved modes of interpreting experience and reality, and for doing this systematically, not only as a result of being fascinated by what is novel but also as a result of prolonged effort; the need not only to discover one's potentialities but also actively to develop them; the need to be realistic in one's self-image, for not all potentialities can be developed and we have to make choices; etc. These must become felt needs if they are to be actual motivators of behavior, and in coping with them the child develops his competencies, skills, intellect, and emotions. All this leads to an expansion of the child's world far beyond what the child left to his own devices (educationally neglected) could ever achieve.
2. There is or is not an adequate *supply* of that which is lacking to gratify the need. Parents are not equally able to provide food, give security and love, or supply intellectual stimulation and linguistic interaction; there may not be enough schools, or there may be inadequate educational provision within the schools. The mere availability of the supply, however, is not enough; it is not a matter of quantity only but of quality as well.
3. There is or is not *support* for the child's efforts to satisfy his own needs. If there is support, it may still be inadequate in a variety of ways: either too much or too little, not adapted to the child's own powers at a particular stage in his development, or inconsistent and thus confusing to the child. Insofar as the intention of the support given is to help the child satisfy his needs in more mature ways (and this would include confronting the child with appropriate new situations and tasks that create new needs in him), we can speak of *educational support*.

If this analysis is correct, it follows that the gratification of needs does not automatically lead to the emergence of new needs and that the path that leads from preoccupation with physiological needs up the ladder to the need for self-actualization is not an inevitable one.

MASLOW, ROUSSEAU, AND
THE EDUCATIONAL ENVIRONMENT

Despite the fact that Maslow has considered needs in relation to the desired end result of personality development, he is still very close to Rousseau in conceiving of a natural development that will unfold, provided the society is "in order" and the educator conceives of his role as that of midwife. This is evident in such statements as:

Self-actualization, the coming to full development and actuality of the potentialities of the organism, is much more akin to growth and maturation than it is to habit formation or association by reward, that is, it is not acquired from without but is rather an unfolding from within of what is in a subtle sense, already there.[17]

The view developed in this chapter would lead us to place greater emphasis on what comes "from without"—the adults, who care for the child and help him expand his own feelings, his needs, his understandings, and his possibilities of choice and action.

We said earlier that Maslow's conception of the mature person is culture- and *Zeitgeist*-bound too but that it is valuable for precisely that reason, for it points up significant aspirations of human beings in our culture today. We should not, however, allow ourselves to be carried away by the vision of self-actualization and fulfillment of ever-greater human potential and creativity without reminding ourselves that maturity can take many forms and involves a wide range of behaviors beyond those specifically mentioned by Maslow. As Langeveld has pointed out in a book dealing with the projective testing of children, "the emphasis cannot be laid primarily or exclusively upon *self*-realization anywhere. It is precisely the mature person who must face up to the relationship 'self-society,' 'self-future,' 'self-past,' after a long history of this 'self' in which it had to take shape."[18]

We turn now from the child's needs to consideration of what it means for the child to be born into a particular society and culture.

Topics for
Further Exploration

1. We have referred to nonreflective care of children, which is rooted
in custom, and to more self-conscious care of children, guided by what
"the experts" recommend. Observe some families with babies and young
children, note which books and articles on child rearing they consult, and
try to assess, from observing what the parents actually do, to what extent
they are really influenced by the advice of "experts." Are there dangers
in relying too much on what "science" teaches?
2. In the light of the theory of needs developed in this chapter, analyze
the needs of children coming to school from severely disadvantaged homes
and communities, and look at what the teacher might do to help these
children satisfy some of their needs and to create new, growth-promoting
needs.
3. Looking at the youth scene today and the disenchantment of many
young people in the schools, analyze what you think are some of the
needs the school often neglects.

References and Comments

1. Lawrence K. Frank, *On the Importance of Infancy* (New York:
    Random House, 1966), p. 62.
2. Margaret Mead, *Coming of Age in Samoa*, first published 1928;
    Growing Up in New Guinea, first published 1930; both now avail-
    able in Penguin Books.
3. Magdalen King-Hall, *The Story of the Nursery* (London: Routledge
    & Kegan Paul, 1950).

    Paul Bode, "Land, Landkind und Landjugend," in *Handbuch der
    pädagogischen Milieukunde*, ed. A. Busemann (Halle a. S.:
    Schroedel, 1932).
4. For an analysis of changes in ideas about child rearing in the United
    States, see Martha Wolfenstein, "Fun Morality: An Analysis of
    Recent American Child-Training Literature," in *Childhood in Con-
    temporary Cultures*, eds. Mead and Wolfenstein (Chicago: Uni-
    versity of Chicago Press, 1955), pp. 168–178. Wolfenstein analyzes
    the *Infant Care* bulletins of the U.S. Department of Labor Children's
    Bureau dated 1914, 1921, 1929, 1938, 1942, 1945, and 1951.
5. C. Kluckhohn and H. A. Murray, *Personality in Nature, Society and
    Culture*, 2d ed., rev. and enl. (New York: Knopf, 1953).

R. Linton, *The Cultural Background of Personality* (New York: Appleton, 1945).

J. Whiting and I. Child, *Child Training and Personality: A Comparative Study* (New Haven: Yale University Press, 1953).

Beatrice B. Whiting, ed., *Six Cultures: Studies of Child Rearing* (New York: Wiley, 1963).

6. Note the comment made by Nico Frijda and Gustav Jahoda "On the Scope and Methods of Cross-Cultural Research," *International Journal of Psychology* 1 (1966):109–127, under the heading "Critique of the Older Conceptual Framework," where they refer specifically to Whiting: "Even in a relatively stable traditional society child-rearing practices merely need to be such as to produce a range of personality types which is not inconsistent with major cultural demands; and considering the complexity of the problems involved, this leaves far more room for variations in personality than a single moulding into shape would imply."

7. D. W. MacKinnon, "The Nature and Nurture of Creative Talent," *American Psychologist* 17 (July 1962).

W. H. O. Schmidt, "The Scientist in the Child and the Child in the Scientist, Some Reflections on the Psychology of Creativity," *Theoria*, University of Natal, no. 22 (1964):43–56.

8. A. H. Maslow, *Motivation and Personality* (New York: Harper & Row, 1954).

9. Books and pamphlets on child rearing written for parents commonly do this too. The *Infant Care* bulletins analyzed by Martha Wolfenstein (op. cit.) illustrate this very well. The conceptions of human nature reflected in the advice given to parents in 1914 and that given after 1940 are in many ways diametrically opposed, but the authors of 1914 seem to take for granted that their conceptions will be shared, and the authors after 1940 also take their own conceptions for granted. With regard specifically to the child's *needs*, we find in 1914 a clear distinction between needs and wants: Wants of the child are not trusted—they are the source of trouble. In 1942–1945 we find an identification of needs and wants: What the child wants is "probably" also what he needs. Cf. also Urie Bonfenbrenner, *Two Worlds of Childhood: U.S. and U.S.S.R.* (New York: Russell Sage, 1970).

10. J. Gay and N. Cole, *The New Mathematics in an Old Culture* (New York: Holt, Rinehart & Winston, 1967).

11. But we needn't look back as far as the seventeenth century. We

again refer to the *Infant Care* bulletins in which Wolfensten (op. cit., pp. 172–173) reports that in 1914 "the dangerousness of play is related to that of the ever present sensual impulses which must be constantly guarded against"; by 1929–1938 "play, having ceased to be wicked, having become harmless and good, now becomes a new duty."

12. See K. Goldstein, *The Organism: A Holistic Approach to Biology Derived from Pathological Data in Man* (New York: American Book, 1939), pp. 196–197. "We can say, an organism is governed by the tendency to actualize, as much as possible, its individual capacities, its 'nature', in the world. . . . This tendency to *actualize 'itself,' is the basic drive, the only drive by which the life of the organism is determined.* This tendency undergoes in the *sick* human being a characteristic change. . . . The tendency to maintain the existent state is characteristic for sick people and is a sign of anomalous life, of decay of life. The tendency of normal life is toward activity and progress. . . . An organism is normal and healthy, in which the tendency towards self-actualization is acting from within, and overcomes the disturbance arising from the clash with the joy of conquest."

13. If taken literally, the statement "what a man can be—he must be" is absurd. I can be a selfish exploiter of other people, but must I be? In the context of everything Maslow has said, this is obviously not what he means. His description of the mature personality implies that mere adaptation to an existing reality is not enough; mature people transcend that reality by being open to new experiences and insights, and facing up to the implications.

14. Maslow, op. cit., p. 283.

15. Maslow, ibid., p. 84.

16. W. H. O. Schmidt, "Conceptions of Human Nature—Potentialities of Human Development," *Theoria*, University of Natal (1968).

17. Maslow, op. cit., p. 107.

18. M. J. Langeveld, *The Columbus: Picture Analysis of Growth Towards Maturity* (Basel and New York: S. Karger, 1969), p. 61.

CHAPTER 4

Man as Animal Symbolicum

Human nature, according to Plato, is like a difficult text, the meaning of which has to be deciphered by philosophy. But in our personal experience this text is written in such small characters that it becomes illegible. The first labour of philosophy must be to enlarge these characters.[1]

Ernst Cassirer

We have described society and culture as a realm other than that of biological inevitability. In this chapter we shall specify the meaning of this statement a little more closely and look at some of its implications for child development. This will be done in two stages: First we shall expound Cassirer's analysis of the *symbolic nature* of the world man has created and, by drawing on what Cassirer says as well as referring to more recent exponents of modern linguistics, give a few indications of characteristics of language systems that seem particularly relevant to an evaluation of the implications for child development of "learning to speak." After this we shall try to trace the nature of the change that occurs in the growing infant and child when it *discovers* and *begins to acquire* language, the supreme but not sole symbolic system.

THE SYMBOLIC WORLD

One might ask why, in a book on child development, we introduce the fundamental ideas of a philosopher of culture on man's creation of a world of symbols. Why not simply take man's ability to form symbols as a fact too obvious to need belaboring and proceed immediately with describing the stages in which the child "learns" language or in which his command of language "grows"? The answer is twofold. In the first place, language occupies a very special place in the development of a child, and we need to articulate some of the salient characteristics of the complex phenomenon "language" before we can describe in any significant way how it is acquired by the child and in what sequence it is acquired. In the second place, and possibly more important, only by dealing with man's capacity for symbol formation at a fundamental level and with the *consequences for culture* written in large characters (as Cassirer's reference to Plato suggests) are we likely to become sufficiently aware of the *consequences for the child* of everything that promotes or hinders his language development and thus to feel sufficiently impelled to pay special attention to the child's acquisition of language.

Very briefly, the argument with regard to the importance of language to the child's development runs as follows: Access to language presupposes active participation and involvement in a world of shared human meanings and in the culture of the group to which the child belongs, and is therefore central to the child's "socialization" and "enculturation." It affects the child's emotional development, because linguistic expression transforms emotional experience. It affects the child's cognitive development, because language not only follows but also anticipates and guides cognitive activity. Finally, defective development of speech and language, whatever its cause—isolation and neglect, sensory and neurological pathology such as in deafness and aphasia, distortion and confusion as a result of a pathological family environment such as Theodore Lidz has described[2]—means much more than a deficit in one function of a biological organism: It always involves for the child the risk of missing the specifically *humanizing* aspect of human development.

Ernst Cassirer has developed his views in a number of writings, the most concise of which is his book *Essay on Man*, which summarizes and sharpens much of what he has said in three massive volumes entitled *The Philosophy of Symbolic Forms*.[3]

Cassirer begins by discussing man as *animal rationale*, a conception dating back to Aristotle. Rationality is supposed to be man's distinguishing characteristic. This rationality, it is held, has enabled man to extend his "natural," "biological," "organic" development.

The relationship of man to his environment is held to be different from that of animals below the level of man. Here Cassirer makes use of the studies of the biologist J. von Uexküll.[4] According to Von Uexküll, each organism below the level of man is adapted to and fitted into its natural environment; each species has its own *Umwelt* (literally: "surrounding world"). Von Uexküll speaks of the "functional circle" of the animal, which defines the scope and limits of the *Umwelt* of each species. This functional circle must be seen in terms of an animal's receptor system (by means of which it receives stimuli of a certain kind from its environment) and its effector system (by which it reacts to the stimuli), the receptor and effector systems being closely linked to form the functional circle. Man has his functional circle too, but his rationality has enabled him to extend it—to create "artificially" civilizations and cultures that have transformed the "natural" environment in which human beings live and children grow up. Thus, man has no fixed *Umwelt*; he is constantly creating and re-creating his own world.

Human beings tend to have ambivalent attitudes toward what their rationality has enabled them to create. Some thinkers have been impressed by the wonder of man's creations, others by their "artificiality" and even depravity. For Rousseau in the eighteenth century, man was a depraved animal who had evolved a civilization and a society, which, instead of allowing "original nature" to develop, distorted and suppressed it. His image of the "noble savage" reflects this view. Rousseau, however, was by no means the last person to yearn for a state of nature. The truth is that whenever people take stock of what man has created, they will inevitably take fright at some of the audacious, stupid, and evil things he has done. But this does not alter the fact that everywhere man has created civilizations and continues to do so, and that it is into some civilization, society, and culture that a child is born. No child can escape the history of the society and culture into which he is born. There is no state of nature, no "Golden Age," except in myth and in the dreams of people who would like to escape from the complexities of their civilization. This is not to say that utopias, myths, and dreams are not powerful factors in bringing about change in a society; indeed they are.

Cassirer then gives a reinterpretation of the conception of man as a rational animal, and this reinterpretation is of great importance to us for understanding the task of the developing child in relation to the culture into which he is born. To describe man as a rational animal, says Cassirer, is valid but one sided. It takes a part for its whole, for man's rationality is part of something wider and more fundamental: the ability to form symbols. He therefore describes man as *animal symbolicum*, the animal that creates symbols and builds up a world of symbols. Language is a symbolic system, but so are mythology, religion, art, mathematics, and science. Each of these symbolic systems has its own inherent possibilities.

The human being is not only faced with a natural environment and the extension of that environment but also with the products of man's symbolic activities. Cassirer stresses the inability of the individual human being to escape from the symbolic world man has created. It is worth quoting at some length a passage from his *Essay on Man* in which he formulates this concept, because it leads us to a deeper understanding of what is involved in what is often too glibly referred to as the socialization and enculturation of the child:

Man cannot escape from his own achievement. He cannot but adopt the conditions of his own life. No longer in a merely physical universe, man lives in a symbolic universe. Language, myth, and religion are parts of this universe. They are the varied threads which weave the symbolic net, the tangled web of human experience. All human progress in thought and experience refines upon and strengthens its net. No longer can man confront reality immediately: he cannot, as it were, see it face to face. Physical reality seems to recede in proportion as man's symbolic activity advances. Instead of dealing with things themselves man is in a sense constantly conversing with himself. He has so enveloped himself in linguistic forms, in artistic images, in mythical symbols or religious rites that he cannot see or know anything except by interposition of this artificial medium. His situation is the same in the theoretical as in the practical sphere. Even here man does not live in the world of hard facts, or according to his immediate needs and desires. He lives rather in the midst of imaginary emotions, in hopes and fears, in his fantasies and dreams.[5]

Cassirer speaks of man without distinguishing between the world of the child and that of the adult. For our purposes we must make this distinction. A child is born *into* a particular society, in a particular civilization, in a particular culture, and at a particular point in historical time. For the infant as distinct from the adult, it is true to say that he *is* confronted by reality in an immediate way. The infant is still characterized by what Schachtel calls "openness to the world"[6] or, as in Langeveld, "open communication with the world."[7] This implies that his relationship to objects, events, and experiences is not yet fixed and ordered in terms of the symbol systems of his culture. But the symbolic systems are nevertheless inescapable for the child, for he cannot be enculturated or realize his potentiality as a human being except by sharing the symbolic world through which the society of which he is a member interprets reality and human experience. It is the "symbolic net, the tangled web of human experience" of his own culture that every child has to unravel anew and discover and re-create for himself. It is in this process of discovering and re-creating that the developing child gives meaning to his own experiences and gives to them an individual as well as shared human significance; thus, the individual, personal element is inextricably interwoven with the cultural. Only *within* the symbolic systems that limit the child's freedom by imposing pattern and already developed meanings on him, and by forcing him to interpret his experience in terms of the possibilities inherent in the symbolic systems, can he become creative. The symbolic system *par excellence* is language.

Man's ability and the child's ability to form symbols depends, of course, on a psychoneurological substrate and, thus, on biologically given equipment. Ashley Montagu refers to this when he says, in connection with the implications of the prolonged dependence of the child on the adult:

Were the anthropoid apes characterized by a period of dependent infancy which was ten times as long as that of man's, they would still not develop anything resembling human culture, since they do not possess the necessary neuropsychic potentialities. The length of the infancy period *in the absence of such potentialities* has a limited significance for the development of culture [italics added].[8]

But there is nothing psychoneurologically or biologically inevitable about acquiring language: Language can only be discovered and acquired by the child in a cooperative situation in which an urge to communicate is aroused and is then directed and channeled by increasing usage of the resources of an already existing language. Nor is there anything biologically inevitable about the differences between existing languages.

A LITTLE LINGUISTICS; A LOT OF LANGUAGE

In describing language as a system, we can distinguish, following Halliday, McIntosh, and Strevens,[9] between the substance, the form, and the context of language. The substance is the "raw material" of language: In spoken language there is a *phonic* substance—that is, it has sounds and phonic patterns. The form refers to *grammar*, including *syntax*, and *lexis*, or vocabulary. The context refers to the relation of form, or internal patterns, to nonlinguistic features of the context in which language operates—that is, to what is usually called *semantics*. In describing the learning of language by the child and the impact of language as a symbolic system on the development of the child, we have to say something about each of these.

　　Language makes use of sounds, but sounds themselves are obviously not language. The small infant gurgling and babbling happily is producing sounds; these sounds may be uttered simply because it is enjoyable to produce them, or they may even "express" a state of relaxed contentment. The crying of a baby is also not language, though it may communicate something to the mother. In saying this we are not denying that this production of sounds by the infant is important to the development of speech in the child and to the eventual acquisition of the language system of his cultural group. M. M. Lewis has written a detailed and fascinating review of the significance of these and related phenomena in early infant development that play a decisive role in the development of speech and the discovery of language by the child.[10] It is possible even for language not to make use of sounds; deaf-mutes can acquire a visual sign language, but this, as we know, can never fully replace the spoken and heard language.[11]

In any language a limited number of sounds, technically known as *phonemes*, enter into the construction of words. How limited these all-important phonemes are is indicated by the following figures quoted by Martinet: In French there are 31 to 34 phonemes; in Spanish and Castilian Spanish, 24; in Spanish as spoken in America, 22. In English, according to Lefevre, there are between 31 and 33 (excluding the 12 significant features of pitch, stress, and juncture).[12]

Languages not only differ with regard to the range of their phonemes but also have their own distinctive phonemic systems. In English, for instance, the length of the vowel *a* in a word does not change its meaning, whereas in some other languages it does. In Mandarin (the form of Chinese now mandatory for all persons in the People's Republic of China) both pitch and tone, and combinations of these, vary the meaning. This does not imply that some of the acoustic features of an utterance, which in English do not form part of the phonemic system of a language, may not color the whole manner in which the speaker speaks and thereby tell us something about his mood, emotion, and intent: For example, a high pitch (in English, anyway) may indicate excitement and alarm.

A language not only has its characteristic system of phonemes but, possibly more important, also has its characteristic patterns of word stress and intonation that affect meaning. However, intonation is not only an essential part of speaking in order to be objectively understood (the referential meaning) but also necessary to convey one's *mood* or *emotional undertone*. We thus have intonation as an aspect of the linguistic system (with its own rules, specific to each language) and intonation as a form of human expression or expression of affect. D. B. Fry stresses the importance to the infant of intonation as the transmitter of affect:

One of the aspects of speech that the child learns to reproduce
quite early is the intonation of what is said to him. This is not
because rises and falls in pitch are particularly easy to imitate but
rather because intonation is closely linked with the affective side
of speech; its use grows naturally out of the expressive sounds the
child has been making, and the emotional tie between mother and
baby ensures that the baby will readily imitate the mood and
tone of the mother.[13]

It is this dual character of intonation—being rooted in spontaneous expression of affect as well as anchored to a linguistic system—that makes it so important to the child's acquisition of language.

In learning a new language, one of the greatest difficulties is to pick out the sounds that differentiate meaning; the phonemic system of the language we already know tends to interfere with acquiring that of the language we want to learn. This is well recognized in modern methods of teaching foreign languages. Increasingly, separate manuals of language instruction based on comparative studies of the language already known to the learner and the language to be learned (including the phonological aspects) are being written.

THE DEVELOPMENT OF SPEECH AND LANGUAGE

When we turn to the development of infants, we notice that they soon become capable of producing a great variety of sounds and that they react to the human voice from a very early age.[14] The significant point is that from the beginning the human voice is an important, emotionally charged constituent of interpersonal relationships. Normally the most important interpersonal relationship is, of course, that between mother and child. When we adults reflect on this relationship, we can distinguish many constituents of it: the communication that takes place in feeding (sense of touch), in giving warmth and support, in play, in facial expression and eye contact, in bodily movements, and in signs and gestures. But for the infant the whole interaction forms part of a complex totality. Out of this totality one constituent, the sound of the human voice, gradually becomes differentiated in order to allow verbal language communication to develop.

The sounds the infant itself produces evoke reactions in other people. The most obvious example of this is crying. Other sounds —the vocalization, the babbling, the lalling, and the first more specific sounds like *ma-ma* and *da-da*—often cause the mother and interested spectators to express delighted interest in the infant. Between the ages of 2 and 18 months, most infants produce sounds in great profusion. Few of these could be described as forming part of the language system of the culture to which the child belongs, although there is already a "drift" toward the sounds of the language spoken by the adults. While the whole of the child's early experience is important to what comes later, the decisive step to language proper is usually made somewhere between the ages of 15 and 24 months. This step is not a result of the accumulation of experiences *only* but is in a real sense a discovery: the discovery of language. An interesting point is that when this step is taken, the range of sounds produced by the child is narrowed, sometimes quite suddenly and dramatically, and confined more and more to the phonemes required by the particular language the child hears around him. About this phenomenon more will be said later, when we relate it to another aspect of the child's language development.

We have somewhat loosely used the term *language proper*. We imply by this that much of what is developed up to the age of roughly 15 months (sometimes as late as 2 years or more) may already have certain features of conventional language—for instance, the child may be forming sound patterns that resemble or are identical with those of the conventional language so that they may be regarded as "words" by the parents. On the other hand, something crucial is still missing. What is this?

Several useful distinctions have been made by students of language. One is that between *emotional* and *propositional* language. Sounds uttered may be a direct expression of an emotional state. According to Köhler, chimpanzees have all sorts of sounds by means of which they unmistakably express rage, terror, despair, grief, pleading, desire, playfulness, and pleasure.[15] Cathy Hayes points out that Viki, the little chimpanzee she reared, had a fixed repertoire of sounds that she uttered involuntarily when in certain emotional states.[16] These sounds had not been learned, for they did not resemble the sounds uttered by the humans with whom Viki associated, and there were no other chimpanzees around from whom she could have learned them. Moreover, Viki could not be induced ever to utter them voluntarily in the absence of the appropriate emotion. Such sounds give direct and unpremeditated expression to emotions; they do not designate or describe objects and experiences the way the *word* "rage," for instance, *designates* that emotion but does not give expression to it.

Propositional language designates something: This is quite a different function, and only human language has this function. Even if animals were able to acquire a number of elements of the human language and, in response to long training, make some use of them, the fact remains that only mankind, in an endless series of generations, has been able to develop language as we know it and as a human child can learn it in a year or two after a preparatory period of socialization.

SIGNALS, SYMBOLS, AND SIGNS

Another important distinction is that between a *signal* and a *symbol*. One can condition human beings as well as animals to react to a large number of signals and to discriminate among them. Red, amber, and green lights at street intersections are signals, not symbols; we learn to react to them by stopping, by being on guard, or by going ahead. The sound of a dinner bell is a signal, not a symbol. The well-trained circus animal responds to very fine differences in signals. The dog senses a great many slight variations in the behavior of his master and reacts appropriately. A signal is always tied to a particular concrete situation; outside the context of that situation it can convey no message. A symbol, on the other hand, designates, represents, or means something. Cassirer puts it this way: "Signals and symbols belong to two different universes of discourse: a signal is a part of the physical world of being; a symbol is part of the human world of meaning. Signals are 'operators.' Symbols are 'designators.' Signals, even when understood and used as such, have nevertheless a sort of physical or substantial being; symbols only have a functional value, . . ."[17]

This distinction is not peculiar to Cassirer; it is well recognized in the study of language. Karl Bühler speaks of "Ablösbarkeit der Sprache" (the separability of language): The symbol is separable from the concrete situation, has an independent existence of its own, and can enter into relationships with other symbols.[18] For example, we can say things that have no reference to any objectively observable or "realistic" fact—like speaking of the gods on Mt. Olympus. We can even build constructions without any referents, such as:

"The tem mubbles the bickle promily." We can analyze this sentence gramatically quite easily: subject, predicate, object, adverb; the words have entered into relationships with each other without referring to anything beyond themselves.

The signals of which we have just spoken, as the examples show, can be learned by animals or by humans. From this we must distinguish the signs animals have at their disposal for passing messages to each other. Biologists have taught us not to underestimate the complexity of the sign "language" of animals. The work of Lorenz and von Frisch is probably the best known. Karl von Frisch titled his book, in which he describes the way in which bees communicate information about the source of food, *Bees, Their Vision, Chemical Senses, and Language.*[19] He was able to show that a honeybee, having found a source of food, comes back to the hive and performs a dance that indicates to the other bees the location of the food—that is, the direction and distance from the hive to the food source. Other bees respond to this information and fly to the source of the food; on returning, they also perform a dance to pass on the message to the next lot of bees, who in their turn fly to the source of the food. How does this compare with human language? Benveniste has summarized the result of the comparison:

The essential difference between the method of communication discovered among bees and our human language . . . can be stated summarily in one phrase which seems to give the most appropriate definition: it is not a language but a signal code. All the characteristics of a code are present: the fixity of the subject matter, the invariability of the message, the relation to a single set of circumstances, the impossibility of separating the components of the message, and its unilateral transmission.[20]

By contrast, we can say that the subject matter of human language is boundless, not confined to a single range or merely to a narrow range of information. The response to a human language utterance is not necessarily an action but, much more characteristically, a dialogue. It embodies experience in such a way that it can be passed on endlessly in time and space, not being bound to the concrete, here-and-now situation. It is an "artificial" creation that can be constantly extended and modified, not an innately fixed code or "natural language." Finally, it must be learned anew by each child, because heredity gives the child only the potentiality for learning a new language, not the equipment of a fixed code.[21]

By "language proper," then, we mean language that has developed beyond expressive sounds and gestures, beyond a system of signals that operate within a concrete situation, beyond mere indication of emotional states and intentions and *has begun to articulate itself in a system of symbols* that belong to the human world of meaning. A human adult who has only expressive and signal language—for instance, the deaf-mute who has not had the advantage of a linguistic education such as is available to deaf-mutes today—can communicate with others, but his communication remains much more tied to his emotions and to the immediate and the concrete.

WORDS AND THINGS:
THE CHILD'S USE OF LANGUAGE

The transition from mere emotional expression in sounds, from communication of intentions or wishes by means of movements and gestures, and from action-response to signals to language proper may be fairly gradual or quite sudden. However, it always marks a very important change in the child's orientation to the things and the world around him. At the age of 2 years, we find in most children an intense interest in the names of things, an interest that usually remains strong for several years and leads to a rapid growth in vocabulary. The things around him take on new meaning when he learns their names, and experiences and events become something different when he can pin them down with words. In a sense one builds up the world of objectively existing things by naming them. Without being named they would still exist, but they would be a confusing welter of vague and unidentified entities without a permanent pattern. By naming them *with the words that are the common property of all* (in that particular language group), one is building up not only an objective world but also *a world that one can share with everyone else.* Language helps the child see the world as it is seen by others.

This does not mean the child does not continue to have a subjective, private world that it cannot express in language—just as we as adults have private worlds for which we do not find words. The small child will express much of his subjective, private world in make-believe, play, fantasy, and expressive gestures; that is why one can use the child's play situation, his drawings and paintings, and all his fantasies, however expressed or enacted, to find out what is going on in him and how he sees the world around him in relation to himself and others.

William Stern described the typical discovery at the age of about 2 years that "everything has a name" as one of the great events in a child's life.[22] This is a specific discovery, but it is based on the discovery of language as such. The discovery that "everything has a name" is made evident when the child begins to ask: "Is a?" or something of the sort. This notion has sometimes been criticized as implying that there is always an occasion when the discovery is made quite abruptly; that is, it is regarded as not taking sufficiently into account what has led up to the discovery. Vygotsky, who criticizes Stern on this account, nevertheless also stresses the preoccupation with naming as a particularly significant event in the development of the child, for it marks the discovery of the function of language as such.[23] Another criticism is that Stern seems to imply that the child of 2 is already capable of generalizing about the function of words. M. M. Lewis deals with this criticism very well by saying: "Stern appears to believe that children as early as the second year arrive at this formulated generalization. This would seem to be too adult, too intellectualized a view of cognitive development at this stage; but perhaps Stern means no more than that children behave 'as though' they had made this discovery—*and this we can well accept*" (italics added.)[24]

When the transition from sign language to symbol language is sudden, we can see most clearly what is involved, for the whole behavior of the child is affected. The significance of discovering the naming function of words (and thus coming to the use of symbolic language) is illustrated most dramatically in the development of deaf-mutes. The most striking example recorded is that of Helen Keller, who became deaf and blind at the age of 19 months and acquired language much later. Mrs. Sullivan, her teacher, has recorded what happened when Helen Keller was 7 years of age. Despite the fact that this passage has often been quoted, we will repeat it here because nothing could make the point more movingly or more instructively:

I must write you a little line this morning because something very important has happened. Helen has taken the second great step in her education. She has learnt that everything has a name, and that the manual alphabet is the key to everything she wants to know. . . . This morning, while she was washing, she wanted to know the name for "water." When she wants to know the name of anything, she points to it and pats my hand. I spelled "w-a-t-e-r" and thought no more about it until breakfast. . . . [Later on] we went to the pump house, and I made Helen hold her mug under the spout while I pumped. As the cold water gushed forth, filling the mug, I spelled "w-a-t-e-r" in Helen's free hand. The word coming so close upon the sensation of cold water rushing over her hand seemed to startle her. She dropped the mug and stood as one transfixed. A new light came into her face. She spelt "w-a-t-e-r" several times. Then she dropped on the ground and asked for its name and pointed to the pump and the trellis and suddenly turning round asked for my name. I spelled "teacher." All the way back to the house she was highly excited, and learned the name of every object she touched, so that in a few hours she had added thirty new words to her vocabulary. The next morning she got up like a radiant fairy. She has flitted from object to object, asking the name of everything and kissing me for very gladness. . . . Everything must have a name now. Wherever we go, she asks eagerly for the names of things she has not learned at home. She is anxious for her friends to spell, and eager to teach the letters to everyone she meets. She drops the signs and pantomimes she used before, as soon as she has words to take their place, and the acquirement of a new word affords her the liveliest pleasure. And we notice that her face grows more expressive each day. . . .[25]

What has happened here? Obviously, before this event Helen had already learned some "words" by a slow process of patient teaching and conditioning. Now, however, she has made a discovery: She has discovered the symbolic function of language. This has two consequences: First, whenever she has learned a new word, the earlier signs and pantomimes are no longer necessary; second, her attention is directed toward the possibilities inherent in language, and she acquires new words very rapidly.

In normal language acquisition, the incidents that mark the transition to "language proper" are not so dramatic. But studies of the increase in vocabulary of children do show that, after a period during which words (whose status as language is often dubious) are learned very slowly, there suddenly comes a rapid increase in vocabulary that is kept up for a long time. In different studies the figures quoted vary considerably; such variations depend on a number of factors such as the sample of children chosen, the techniques of observation used, and the criteria for defining what to recognize as a word. To illustrate the general pattern of findings, we shall quote a very conservative estimate of vocabulary growth, arrived at by M. E. Smith in 1926.[26] The children involved were all from middle-class homes in the United States.

Age in months	Number of words	Gain
12	3	—
18	22	19
24	272	250
30	446	174
36	896	450
42	1222	326
48	1540	318
54	1870	330
60	2072	202
66	2289	217
72	2562	273

DISCOVERING, ACQUIRING, AND RE-CREATING

Language does not consist only of isolated words, however; it consists of utterances in which the words occur together. A characteristic of a symbol is that it can be separated from its concrete context and can enter into relationships with other symbols. In every language there are certain patterns, later to be understood as rules, that regulate the manner in which words can be combined: the rules of syntax and grammar. Here again the child comes up against a system that already exists; he discovers it and then gradually acquires it. Discovering it does not mean being able to give a verbal account of it; few adults can formulate the rules by which they form their sentences. It does, however, imply the awareness that there are rules. As children begin to generate more and more utterances, putting together words into phrases and sentences, their utterances begin to conform more and more to the patterns required by the particular language they are learning to speak. Just as children are often enthralled by learning new words, they are often fascinated by experimenting with new ways of combining them.

We have been using the words "discovering" and "acquiring" deliberately to indicate that learning to speak normally involves the child very actively. Language is acquired in a process of active participation with adults, and in the course of the linguistic interaction between adult and child, the child often pays very close attention to how the adult is saying something and then tries out some of the patterns he notices. Several studies in recent years have highlighted the small child's preoccupation with grammatical and syntactic patterns.

Kaper, a Dutch investigator, published a book in 1959 in which he presented language produced by two children over a period of 6 years. A remarkable feature of the children's utterances is that many of them are comments on their own language. Kaper is also able to show convincingly the unintentional influence adults have on children's sentence construction.[27] But the child is not only listening carefully to the way the adult is saying something; quite frequently the child is also inviting the adult, by means of a question, to correct him.

ADAM AND EVE

In 1964 the American investigators Roger Brown and Ursula Bellugi published an account of the acquisition of syntax by two children, Adam and Eve.[28] For 2 hours every second week over a period of 38 weeks, the investigators visited each child and its mother, and took complete tape recordings of everything that was said, noting the context in which what was said occurred. Eve was 18 months old at the beginning of the investigation and Adam 27 months. Among the highly interesting observations the authors make, we find the following:

The mother—probably unwittingly—in speaking to the child and in responding to the child's own statements speaks in short and simple sentences: "For the most part they are the kinds of sentences Adam will produce a year later." The mother provides model sentences (or noun phrases), which the child tries to imitate, often leaving out something in his imitation; conversely, the child says something and the mother expands this into a full sentence.

Examples of the former:

Mother	Child's incomplete imitation
Fraser will be unhappy.	Fraser unhappy
Daddy's brief case.	Daddy brief case

Examples of the latter:

Child	Mother's expansion
Sat wall	He sat on the wall.
Eve lunch	Eve is having lunch.

Brown and Bellugi point out that the incomplete imitations, or reductions, made by the child take a predictable form: (1) The order in which the mother spoke the words will be preserved; (2) the child's imitations will include only nouns, verbs, and sometimes adjectives; and (3) most likely to be omitted are inflections, auxiliary verbs, articles, prepositions, and conjunctions. Nouns, verbs, and adjectives—the words that are retained—are sometimes called *contentives* because what is most striking about them is that they have semantic content. Words belonging to these classes form an "open list" or "open set"; that is, they are extremely numerous and can always be added to. We can convey a message by making use only of these, but unless we know the total context (as when we send a telegram, in which case we also confine ourselves mainly to contentives) the message can easily be misunderstood. The words omitted, on the

other hand, are called *functors* because their most striking characteristic is that they have grammatical functions. They form a "closed
system"; that is, they are limited in number, and there are rules as
to how they operate. Predictions (2) and (3) are based on linguistic
criteria.

On the other hand, the mother's expansion of the child's statement usually cannot be predicted on linguistic grounds alone. The
expansion of "Eve lunch" into "Eve is having lunch" adds the verb
in the present-progressive form; in other words, a choice has been
made between several different forms (simple present, simple past,
past, future, etc.). This depends on the mother's correct interpretation of the experience or observation the child is trying to communicate. For the mother to expand the child's statement adequately
requires, therefore, close rapport between adult and child. The
significance of the expansion by "is having" goes beyond the mere
use of a form that is grammatically correct: In due course the child
will make distinctions about events in the time continuum to which
the different forms of the verb draw his attention.

When the child learns to use correctly the definite article "the"
and the indefinite article "a," he is not only learning correct grammar
according to adult conventions but also learning to make a distinction between a particular instance of a class ("Did you see *the* bird?")
and a general instance of a class ("Did you see *a* bird?"). The fact
that with certain words of the class we call nouns, the indefinite
article is used (a cup, a horse, a car) while for others it is never
used (sand, water, dirt) implies something about the actual differences between the objects referred to: Some are countable, some not.

The choices that the available grammatical alternatives in a
language force upon the speaker have implications for cognition.
"The meanings added by the functors," say Brown and Bellugi,
"seem to be nothing less than the basic terms in which we construe
reality." And a little later they add: "It seems to us that a mother
in expanding speech may be teaching more than grammar; she may
be teaching something like a world-view."

It is not suggested that what has been said about the importance
of the cycle of linguistic interaction between mother and child ex-
hausts all the ways in which the two children made progress in

learning to form sentences. Children seem to be preoccupied with language even in situations where they are not interacting with other people.

LINGUISTIC FORMS FASCINATE

The small child's preoccupation with linguistic forms has recently been illustrated by a fascinating study of the monologues of a 2½-year-old boy, recorded when he was lying in his cot just before going off to sleep. In *Language in the Crib*, Ruth Weir analyzed the material she obtained from tape recordings of the soliloquies of her own son.[29] Some of the sequences of utterances, as Roman Jakobson, a noted linguist, says in a preface to Weir's book, "bear striking resemblance to the grammatical and lexical exercises in text-books for self-instruction in foreign languages." For instance, the following might be called an exercise in pronominal substitutions:

Take the monkey.
Take it.

Don't take it off.
Don't take the glasses off.

Stop it.
Stop the ball.
Stop it.

and the following, an exercise in noun-phrase substitutions:

There's a hat.
There's another.
There's hat.
There's another hat.

Embedded in the sequences of utterances, we can also discern a great deal of play with sounds. In contrast to the pleasure the child takes in sound during the prelanguage stage, now the play also proceeds in a linguistic context, and there it has linguistic consequences. For instance, in a sequence that begins "That's office . . . That's office . . . Look Sophie . . . That Sophie," it seems to be primarily the *s* sound of "office" that leads him on to "Sophie," for "office" and "Sophie" are not related or associated in any other way in his experience. So here the play with sound seems to determine the choice of the word. However, the interest may suddenly shift from the sound to the last thing signified, in this case the real person Sophie, so in the next utterance he tells something about what happened: "Come last night."

SPEECH AND LANGUAGE AS CULTURAL EVENTS

We are now at the point where we can elaborate, as promised earlier, on the statement concerning the narrowing of the range of sounds produced by the child when he starts to speak. "Narrowing" is a very incomplete description of what occurs. There is, as Roman Jakobson has shown in a paper that has become a classic in linguistics,[30] not simply a narrowing; there is also a loss of ability to produce sounds that the child *could* produce before he acquired the phonemic system, in which only certain sounds have functions while others do not. There is, therefore, not just a narrowing but also a focusing on functional units.

When sounds become speech sounds (i.e., part of a language system), their function changes. For the child it is no longer just a matter of recognizing them as sounds but of recognizing them as contrastive elements in a phonemic system. The attitude the child adopts toward those elements can be illustrated by an analogy. A small child may be delighted by the figures on a chessboard and may play with them: He enjoys the smoothness, the varying contours; tests their hardness by knocking them against each other; clutches them in his hand, throws them, or even sucks them. When later he learns to play chess, the same objects only have a function within the system of chess playing. Although the pieces still have qualities that, outside the context of chess playing, can give pleasure to the child (or indeed to the adult), these qualities are irrelevant to the playing of chess, in which the figures have definite functions defined by the purpose and rules of the game. So, too, recognizing and using the sounds of the phonemic system as an integral part of the language system and for the purpose of communication involve an entirely new dimension of relevance. In listening, the child has to make use of acoustic cues only for the purpose of sorting the incoming sounds into the correct phonemic categories—e.g., *p* not *t*, *p* not *d*, *p* not *b*, etc. The acoustic cues do not produce the phonemic system; the phonemic system determines what cues are relevant.

Fry points out that in the reception of speech, all the learning is done by the brain (central nervous system processes), not by the peripheral hearing mechanisms that relay the sound.[31] As he and his associates have demonstrated, even children with minimal hearing can acquire the phonemic system, provided they are stimulated appropriately and early enough. The acquisition of the phonemic system is a cognitive-conceptual task rather than a sensory-discrimination task only. When listening to speech and trying to speak, the child ignores the aspects of sound that are irrelevant to the purpose of language and the "rules of the game." This is why, when he is starting to speak, sounds no longer just tumble out of him (Jakobson cites from the diary of William Preyer the expression "delirium of the tongue"); he is now intent on selecting in accordance with the demands of the system. The early experience in producing expressive sounds and imitating sounds will have given him better control over the purely articulatorymotoric and auditory-feedback aspects of utterance, but control over these now passes to the cognitive-conceptual sphere and the demands of the language system.

Fortunately for the child, his own fascination with language phenomena, supported by a delight in play with sounds, usually ensures the concentration and practice, as the studies by Kaper, Brown and Bellugi, and Weir have illustrated. More than that: While speech does not develop in the absence of a cooperative situation between the child and at least one other person, who cares for him and enables him to get his first glimpse of a language system, acquiring a language is aided by the very fact that it is a system that can be explored, as well as regenerated in each child anew, to become the very fabric and texture of his own personal, yet shared, human experience. This gives to the learning of language a peculiarly creative quality.[32]

Topics for
Further Exploration

1. Over the years there has been a controversy concerning the role of imitation in the child's acquisition of language, and in modern developmental psycholinguistics it has become a crucial issue. Sort out the different arguments by looking up what is said about imitation in the following books:

D. McNeill, *The Acquisition of Language* (New York: Harper & Row, 1970).

D. Slobin, *Psycholinguistics* (Glenview, Ill.: Scott, Foresman, 1971).

Paula Menyuk, *The Acquisition and Development of Language* (Cambridge: M.I.T. Press, 1971).

Compare what they say with what Arthur W. Staats, a neobehaviorist, says about imitation in *Child Learning, Intelligence, and Personality* (New York: Harper & Row, 1971). Are the interpretations reconcilable?

2. In this chapter we have referred to defective development of speech and language but have not elaborated on this. Read S. Kastein and B. Trace, *The Birth of Language—The Case History of a Nonverbal Child* (Springfield, Ill.: C. C. Thomas, 1966). Does this book help you see more clearly some of the conditions necessary for normal speech development to take place? Formulate them.

3. The acquisition of language is not just a matter of labeling; it is also one of playing with sounds and learning intonation. What might a child learn by being exposed to a vast number of nursery and nonsense rhymes? Analyze a number of nursery rhymes in terms of rhythm, meter, rhyme, repetition of phonemes, and the like in order to arrive at an answer.

References and Comments

1. Ernst Cassirer, *Essay on Man* (New Haven: Yale University Press, 1946), p. 63.

2. Theodore Lidz, *The Family and Human Adaptation* (London: Hogarth Press and Institute of Psychoanalysis, 1964).

3. Ernst Cassirer, *The Philosophy of Symbolic Forms*, 3 vols. (New Haven, Conn.: Yale University Press, 1953, 1955, 1957). First ed. in German, *Philosophie der symbolischen Formen*, 3 vols. (Berlin: Cassirer, Bruno, 1923–1929).

4. Jakob von Uexküll, "A Stroll Through the World of Animals and Men," in *Instinctive Behavior: The Development of a Modern Con-

cept, ed. C. H. Schiller (New York: International Universities, 1957).

5. Ernst Cassirer, *Essay on Man,* op. cit., p. 25.

6. E. Schachtel, *Metamorphosis: On the Development of Affect, Perception, Attention, and Memory* (New York: Basic Books, 1959). "While it can be fruitful metaphorically to speak of and describe the *Umwelten* in which the members of a particular civilization, or social class, or group, or, finally, individual people live, these *Umwelten* are essentially different from the animals' *Umwelten* in that they are largely cultural and not instinctbound. They do not, however, constitute all of man's world, because man can and does constantly transcend these *Umwelten* into the infiniteness of the world, thus encountering ever new aspects of world which then, in turn, may become assimilated and, as it were, petrified in becoming institutionalized parts of culture" [n. 33, p. 53].

7. M. J. Langeveld, *Studien zur Anthropologie des Kindes,* 3d ed. (Tübingen: Max Niemeyer Verlag, 1968), p. 143.

8. M. F. Ashley Montagu, *On Being Human* (New York: Hawthorn, 1966), p. 76.

9. M. A. K. Halliday, A. McIntosh, and P. Strevens, *The Linguistic Sciences and Language Teaching* (New York: McKay, 1964).

10. M. M. Lewis, *Language, Thought, and Personality* (London: Harrap, 1963). For greater detail see his *Infant Speech,* 2d ed. (London: Routledge & Kegan Paul, 1951).

11. Tervoort, in Holland, has made a fascinating study of what he calls "esoteric language" in deaf children. See B. Th. M. Tervoort, *Structurele analyse van visueel taalgebruik binnen een groop dowe kinderen* (structural analysis of visual language usage within a group of deaf children) (Zwolle: N. V. Noord-Hollandse Uitgevers Maatschappij, 1953); the book contains a summary in English in vol. 1, p. 293.

12. A. Martinet, *Elements of General Linguistics* (London: Faber and Faber, 1964). First published in French in 1960.

   O. A. Lefevre, *Linguistics and the Teaching of Reading* (New York: McGraw-Hill, 1964).

13. D. B. Fry, "The Development of the Phonological System in the Normal and the Deaf Child," in *The Genesis of Language,* eds. F. Smith and G. A. Miller (Cambridge, Mass.: M.I.T. Press, 1966).

14. See Lewis, *Language, Thought, and Personality,* op. cit., p. 14: "We have, then, already in a child's earliest weeks the two con-

vergent groups of factors that will continue throughout his linguistic growth: the child utters sounds and responds to the human voice, his mother responds to his sounds and speaks to him."

15.   W. Köhler, *The Mentality of Apes*. Available in Pelican Books, 1957, but first published in English in 1925. First published in German in 1917.

16.   Cathy Hayes, *The Ape in Our House* (New York: Harper & Row, 1951).

17.   Cassirer, *Essay on Man*, op. cit., p. 32.

18.   Karl Bühler, *Sprachtheorie. Die Darstellungsfunktion der Sprache*, 2d printing (Stuttgart: G. Fischer, 1964). Originally published in 1934.

19.   Karl von Frisch, *Bees, Their Vision, Chemical Senses, and Language* (Ithaca, N.Y.: Cornell University Press, 1950).

20.   Quoted by Jacques Maritain in "Language and the Theory of the Sign," in *Language: An Enquiry into Its Meaning and Function*, ed. R. N. Anshem (New York: Harper & Row, 1957), p. 91.

21.   See Benveniste, in Maritain, op. cit.

22.   W. Stern, *Psychologie der frühen Kindheit*, 9th ed. (Heidelberg: Quelle und Meyer, 1967). First ed. in 1914. There is an English translation of the 3d ed., *Psychology of Early Childhood* (London: Allen and Unwin, 1924).

23.   L. S. Vygotsky, *Thought and Language* (Cambridge, Mass.: M.I.T. Press, 1962).

24.   Lewis, *Language, Thought, and Personality*, op. cit., p. 90.

25.   Quoted by Cassirer in *Essay on Man*, op. cit., p. 84. Originally quoted in Helen Keller, *The Story of My Life* (New York: Doubleday, 1902–1903). Supplementary Account of Helen Keller's Life and Education, pp. 315 ff.

26.   M. E. Smith, "Language Development," chap. 9 in *Handbook of Child Psychology*, ed. Carl Murchison (Worcester, Mass.: Clark University Press, 1931).

27.   W. Kaper, *Kindersprachforschung mit Hilfe des Kindes. Einige Erscheinungen der kindlichen Spracherwerbung erläutert im Lichte des vom Kinde gezeigten Interesses für Sprachliches* (Research into child language with the help of the child. Some aspects of language acquisition interpreted in the light of the interest shown by the child in linguistic phenomena) (Groningen: J. B. Wolters, 1959).

28.   R. Brown and Ursula Bellugi, "Three Processes in the Child's Acquisition of Syntax," *Harvard Educational Review* 34 (1964):

133–151. For other accounts of the acquisition of syntax, see R. Brown, "The Acquisition of Syntax," *Monographs of Society for Research in Child Development* 29 (1964):43–79; R. Brown and C. Fraser, "The Acquisition of Syntax," in *Verbal Behavior and Learning*, eds. C. N. Cofer and B. S. Musgrave (New York: McGraw-Hill, 1963).

29. Ruth Weir, *Language in the Crib* (The Hague: Mouton, 1962).

30. R. Jakobson, *Child Language Aphasia and Phonological Universals*, trans. A. R. Keiler (The Hague: Mouton, 1968). Originally published in German, *Kindersparche, Aphasie, und allgemeine Lautgesetze* (Uppsala: Almqvist & Wiksell, 1941).

31. F. Smith and G. A. Miller, eds., *The Genesis of Language* (Cambridge, Mass.: M.I.T. Press, 1966), pp. 197–199.

32. G. A. Miller writes, in "Foreword by a Psychologist," in Weir's book, op. cit., p. 15: "After many years of reading psychological theories about the environmental events that strengthen or weaken various stimulus-response associations, I was completely unprepared to encounter a two-year-old boy who—all alone—corrected his own pronunciations, drilled himself on consonant clusters, and practised substituting his small vocabulary into fixed sentence frames. The gap between this child's reported behavior and all I had been led to expect from the books of Pavlov, Watson, Thorndike, Hull, and other association theorists was more than I knew how to cope with. If you read Dr. Weir's report with an eye for how you might build an explanation in terms of rewarding or punishing stimulus-response connections, you may get some feeling for the difficulties that young Anthony poses for the psychological theory of human learning."

Brown and Bellugi, op. cit., p. 151, in discussing an aspect of the acquisition of syntax that we have not described—"the induction of latent structure"—make this comment: "It looks as if this last process will put serious strain on any learning theory thus far conceived by psychology."

CHAPTER 5

The Child's Conception of Natural Phenomena and Science

No Columbus, no Marco Polo has ever seen stranger and more fascinating and thoroughly absorbing sights than the child that learns to perceive, to taste, to smell, to touch, to hear and see, and to use his body, his senses, and his mind. No wonder that the child shows an insatiable curiosity. He has the whole world to discover. Education and learning, while on the one hand furthering this process of discovery, on the other hand gradually brake and finally stop it completely. There are relatively few adults who are fortunate enough to have retained something of the child's curiosity, his capacity for questioning and for wondering.[1]

    Ernest G. Schachtel

By describing the child's development of interest in and his interpretation of natural events, we can illustrate many of the points made in the previous chapters. At the same time, this chapter is intended as preparation for the more systematic discussion of cognitive development set forth in the following chapter. A brief recapitulation highlighting these points is in order.

CHILD-ADULT INTERACTION

Whatever a child becomes and what he becomes capable of is not simply the result of an assumed natural development (see Chapter 1). The growth and development of any child, except the completely neglected one (and this no society tolerates), takes place in an on-going interactive situation between the child (as educand) and the parent, guardian, teacher, or other adult (as educator). The educator acts for the child where the child cannot yet act for himself; he structures the environment for the child so that the child can make sense of it and cope with it; he lets the child be confronted with ever-new aspects of reality, as he sees it, and shields the child from premature confrontation with tasks and experiences that might overwhelm the child; he supports the child's own efforts to comprehend or master or enjoy the ever-larger world of which the child becomes aware and is *made* aware (see Chapters 2 and 3). That larger world includes the symbolic worlds, through which and in terms of which the experience of the individual is interpreted (see Chapter 4).

This does not imply complete cultural determinism: The symbolic systems are themselves subject to change by individuals, who use them in their own individual ways. It does imply, though, that one of the most important things the educator does is to make available to the educand something of what the culture has to offer: its language; its interpretation of natural events and the cosmos; its patterning of social behavior and interpretation of human relationships; its forms of music, art, recreation, work, etc. Hence, *what* aspects of reality the individual child is likely to pay attention to and explore, and *in what ways*, will be greatly determined by what aspects of the culture his educators make available. Some of this will be made available through deliberate instruction; a great deal will be conveyed by example and without reflection.

The child, on his part, is not a passive receptacle for information. His acquisition of language is best described as a process of re-creation: The child is very active in acquiring language. He asserts his own wants, desires, intentions, interests, interpretations, and autonomy. In the interaction between educand and educator, too, the child is very much an active agent. Nevertheless, it is with the help of the educator—often in response to what the educator makes available—that the child increases his own power to explore the world and to make it meaningful to himself, as well as to cope with its demands and stresses and strains.

At a particular stage in his development, the child may have needs that have priority over everything else at that time. Unless these needs are satisfied or rendered less urgent by the emergence or creation of new, more growth-promoting needs, these unsatisfied needs may prevent him from exploring and interpreting more aspects of reality (see Chapter 3).

THE CHILD AND NATURAL PHENOMENA

We come, then, to the young child's interest in and interpretation of natural phenomena. In this connection the term *spontaneous forma-tion* is often used. By spontaneous formation of scientific concepts, we refer to the formation of concepts in relation to natural phenomena and occurrences that engage the attention of the child in the course of his ordinary encounters with his environment; it is said to be the result of activity initiated by the child himself.

By implication, there is also *nonspontaneous formation* of con-cepts, which takes place not in the course of the child's ordinary, unplanned encounters with natural phenomena but as a result of deliberate, planned teaching, which induces, guides, and regulates the formation of his concepts. We have to be cautious, however, in implying such a contrast. The need for caution will become evident toward the end of this chapter.

The word "scientific" in this context is intended to mean "relating to natural phenomena with which the sciences also deal" as well as "looking for an explanation of how the natural phenomenon comes about or how it is related to other phenomena." It is necessary to say this, because in the child's—and for that matter the adult's—relation to objects, including natural phenomena, the aspect under which the object is experienced may have nothing to do with its explanation as a natural phenomenon in the realm of science.[2] To the poet, to the scientist, and to the interpreter of projective tests, a tree is three very different things; the soap bubbles a child blows are likely to be experienced not so much as something requiring an explanation but as objects of beauty being produced by the child himself to be enjoyed.

If we want to see how natural phenomena and occurrences engage the attention of the child in the course of ordinary encounters with his environment, we must observe individual children making those encounters within their own individual worlds over reasonably long periods of time. We need the sort of carefully recorded observation on the development of individual children that, with regard to language development, we get in the diaries of Leopold, Lewis, Scupin, and Stern:[3] Only the focus should be specifically on the child's encounters with and explanations of natural phenomena.

Now, it is striking that documentation in the form of carefully kept diaries concentrating specifically on the child's explanations of natural phenomena is very scanty. No doubt one reason for this is that the methodological problems involved in making such observations and recording them are formidable. Unfortunately, controlled experimentation with children is no substitute; it is a supplement and a refinement, enabling us to probe into aspects of the child's development of concepts once we know what aspects have revealed themselves in the course of an individual child's ordinary—not experimentally controlled—encounters with his environment. As experimentation becomes more and more removed from the ordinary situations in which a child lives his own life, it is all too easy to lose one's grip on the whole context in which the child ordinarily becomes aware of natural phenomena and on how he deals with this awareness and *how he is helped to deal with it.* For an important feature of the child's world is that he is dependent on and interacting with adults, who structure the environment for him and help him clarify his own experiences.

THE DEVELOPMENT OF SCIENTIFIC CONCEPTS

To illustrate some of the features of so-called spontaneous development of scientific concepts, we shall make extensive use of John G. Navarra's book *The Development of Scientific Concepts in a Young Child.*[4] It is, to our knowledge, the only fairly recent and sufficiently detailed record specifically concentrating on an individual child's encounters with natural phenomena over a sufficiently long period.

The record is based on the observation of a boy named L. B.

from the age of 3 until he was just over 5 years of age. His mother was the observer and recorder, while his father was the investigator. The intelligence of the boy was tested when he was 4 years and 7 months old, and his unstipulated numerical score was described as "high average"; he was not an unusually intelligent child in terms of test performance. His vocabulary at that stage was well developed: We are told that there was only one word in a vocabulary test for 8-year-old children that he did not know. However, we are also informed that he showed more interest and attention when he had to deal with concrete situations than when he was asked questions about words. This would be typical of children of his age. L. B. was an only child.

The situations in which the child was observed were typical daily activities, not experimentally created situations. These were, more than anything else, play situations: play with other children, play alone, play with father or mother or both or merely in their presence, but also story-telling situations, looking at television, going for walks in New York. On the rich source of material from play situations, Navarra writes:

During play the child seemed to become self-involved in meaningful activity. That is, at times he devoted long periods to an activity in which he was engaged. He also became completely engrossed in what he was doing. The child concentrated! It might be suggested that this concentration was probably due to the quality of meaning this activity had from the point of view of the child. Basically this was the assumption upon which the decision to study the child through such activity was based. The study of play activity became the most important device by which insight was gained concerning the conceptual development of the child.[5]

The method of recording was stenographic, and there were quite a few photographs. What was recorded was what the child said, what he did, and as much of the total situation as possible. Altogether more than 4500 entries were made, supplemented by pictures; over a period of roughly 2 years, this amounts to an average of just over six records per day. The book by Navarra is based on these records, from which only extracts plus interpretation are published.

We need to know something about one further, and quite crucial, item pertaining to the world in which the child was growing up and having his experiences: We must know about his parents, and particularly about the relationship between parents and child. The father and mother were well-educated people: The father was studying for a higher degree in education at the time and had undertaken this investigation in order to meet a requirement of the degree he sought. We have, therefore, a child from a home in which a certain characteristic orientation toward knowledge as such prevailed; moreover, the parents were particularly interested in the specific facet of the child's development that was to be investigated. As in the diaries of the language development of individual children, we are therefore dealing with a family and a cultural situation that, although not unique, was a special one: Not all children grow up under quite these circumstances. We shall come back to this point later.

As far as the relationship between parents and child is concerned, this was analyzed by Navarra himself, and the quoted records of what went on between parent and child reflect fairly clearly the nature of the relationship and the implicit basic attitudes.

In the first place, it is quite clear that L. B. felt accepted and secure; the parents took seriously everything he did, and he could rely on them. The basic needs for affection and security had been met.

Although limits were set, L. B. had a large measure of freedom—to explore, to play, and to express his ideas. He did a great deal of exploring, and in the course of this he took risks; when this happened, the parents did not communicate their own fears to the child but intervened only when it was quite clear that the risks were too great. Navarra makes the point that many of the most revealing records would not have come about if the parents had intervened whenever risk was involved. The boy was encouraged to go ahead with what he was doing both by the positive interest shown by his parents and by the lack of unnecessary apprehension. L. B., like any other child, "played." He explored, and then "things happened." The child, once provoked by the object, tried to let things happen again or to let other things—unanticipated—happen. Exploration and play were thus directly related.

Another feature was the marked willingness of the parents to listen to the child and to restrain themselves from asking questions prematurely. Navarra makes an interesting comment about this, for it has a bearing on the kind of information often obtained from children who are asked questions in experimental situations: "One might say that the investigators learned not to pressure the child into telling or giving an explanation about anything. In the early phases of the investigation, there were indications that the child could not be hurried into revealing what he was about. On the few occasions when he was put on the spot, superficial replies were obtained. This seemed to indicate that he was not ready to talk."[6]

In answering the child's questions, the parents also exercised considerable restraint: The answers were seldom direct explanations; much more often they were of the type that in therapy would be called "nondirective," mirroring or slightly reformulating the child's question in order to induce him to go just one step further in clarifying his puzzlement or his ideas. Even the most obscure statements by the child seem to have been treated as though there might be something in them, and he was certainly never ridiculed. The reaction of L. B. and his playmates to being observed and to the records being kept seems to be that they accepted all this as a matter of course.

Here, then, we clearly have a child whose basic needs for security and affection have been satisfied and whose parents interact and communicate with him, respect his autonomy, and do not unduly pressure him. We expect such a child to be very active in exploring his little world.

Now, what are some of the significant features of L. B.'s encounters with natural phenomena and his attempts to explain them? They include:

1.   When L. B.'s attention is engaged by a natural phenomenon that momentarily fascinates, frightens, or puzzles him, the matter usually does not rest there—he comes back to it again and again, at varying intervals, over a period of weeks, months, and in one case 1½ years; one might say a *theme* develops.
2.   Usually there is a strong *emotional involvement*; what he has taken note of is something that affects him personally, delights him,

fascinates him, or arouses fear or apprehension in him—without, however, overwhelming him.

3. Quite often the urgency of his concern in the initial stages is very clearly and directly connected with his self-understanding.

4. His verbalizations—i.e., what L. B. says when he is offering an explanation or asking questions—form only a small part of the development of the theme. The other part is enacted in play, in which L. B. is often doing what one can only call experimenting.

5. If we look at the whole theme and see the progressive transformations in the kind and content of the explanations, we are struck by what Navarra calls *expectancy patterns* in the child. L. B. never formulates his expectancy pattern explicitly, but it is there nevertheless and can be inferred from his behavior; when an expectancy pattern lets him down, he becomes very involved emotionally and very active, and this may lead to a new expectancy pattern or to a temporary turning away from the phenomenon in bewilderment.

6. A particular theme may not only have a long life but also broaden out and *connect* up with other themes with totally different points of origin and give rise to new and broader themes.

7. Although the parents restrain themselves from giving ready-made explanations, it becomes quite clear that the language they use and the new words they occasionally introduce often act as focal points that give new direction to his observations and search for explanation, even though the meanings of the words are initially very vague to him.

Two themes out of the very many that Navarra describes must suffice to illustrate at least some of these features. We have chosen one that leads the child into the understanding of biology and another that, at a later stage, will form part of the discipline of physics.

The first one concerns the distinction between living and dead, and how L. B.'s first ideas about death take shape and change. It is necessary first to state that at the age of about 3 years and 4 months, L. B. is making a distinction between "real" and "fake." "Fake" seems to refer to something that is made—a copy of something, not the real thing—such as a savings bank in the form of a pig, an ashtray in the form of a cow, a drawing or a paper cutout that is to represent something else, and even a story, which in one of the entries quoted is referred to as a "fake story." One criterion for distinguishing between real and fake is whether or not the thing can move and initiate movement; as this criterion becomes dominant, stories very soon come to occupy a special place. Here are some examples to illustrate L. B.'s preoccupation with this criterion:

3 Years, 4 Months:

L. B. had just dropped some coins in his pig-bank. It was about 12 in. long and 6 in. high. The eyes were adorned by large painted lashes. L. B. patted the pig and said, "This little pig never opens his eyes."

L. B. picked up an ash tray which was made in the shape of a cow. L. B. examined it, as though talking to himself, said "I know this cow can't walk"—he paused and then continued—"because his feet are stuck together. I would have to cut it here and here." He pointed to the front and rear legs as he made this last statement. Mother inquired, "Can't he walk now?" L. B. replied, "No, first you have to move one and then the other." He illustrated by moving his legs in the process of walking.[7]

3 Years, 7 Months:

L. B. was playing with a rubber knife. L. B. placed the knife in a doll's mouth. Alan, a little friend with whom he was playing, said, "What are you trying to do—make him sick?" L. B. answered, "He can't get sick, 'cause he isn't real. His mouth doesn't open and he can't walk."[8]

The next entry shows L. B. enacting the condition of "not being real":

3 Years, 9 Months:

L. B. threw himself on the floor and remained in this prone position without moving. His mother asked what he was doing and he said, "I'm a statue." Mother jokingly said, "O.K. statue, it's time to get up." L. B. remained on the floor and very seriously replied, "I can't. Statues can't get up." Mother asked, "Why?" L. B., getting up from the floor, said, "Cause their legs aren't real."[9]

The next example needs no comment:

3 Years, 11 Months:

Mother had been out shopping, and when she returned she told
L. B. that "real bunnies" were being sold in the pet shop for
Easter. L. B. became very excited and said, "You mean their eyes
open and shut and their legs can move and they can walk?"[10]

This criterion for real things soon comes to play an important
role also in distinguishing between *alive* and *dead*. When his pet
turtle does not move despite some prodding, L. B. (at 3 years and 5
months) immediately jumps to the conclusion that the turtle is dead.
The same thing happens when he sees a goldfish motionless in a
bowl. As this preoccupation grows, L. B. and his playmates develop
a favorite form of play: "I'm dead. I can't move." It takes many
forms and becomes more elaborate: For instance, they roll down a
hill, and when they arrive at the bottom they have to be dead. Very
soon they start competing to see who can be dead longest. And then
L. B. wants to know: If one is dead, can one ever move again? At
this stage an elderly woman known to him dies.

When L. B. heard of the death, he asked if he could see her. One
of the first things he asked was, "Will she be dead long?" He
momentarily accepted an explanation of the permanence of death,
but once he and his mother were alone L. B. asked, "Won't she *ever*
be able to move?" The idea of permanency recurred many times,
and seven weeks later L. B. asked, "Is Mrs. Z still dead?"[11]

If locomotion is the basis for distinguishing between fake and
real, and also between alive and dead, then the question arises: What
is the relationship between real and dead? L. B. formulates this
question himself: "What happens to you when you die—aren't you
real any more?"

Locomotion is the first criterion by which L. B. distinguishes between dead and alive, and from locomotion in general he gradually
differentiates movements of parts of the body. He wants to know
whether dead people defecate (he asks this question while busy with
this activity himself), urinate, see, or talk after death; then come
questions about the heart and breathing. It is as if, as he identifies
more and more of the activities of his own living body, he were trying to experience at the same time what it implies to be dead.

He also becomes interested in what seems at first to play no role: what causes death. His first notion seems to come from watching cowboy shows on television, for he asks: "Can you die if you're not shot?" Then gradually illness comes to be linked with death, and when he or someone else falls ill, he asks: "Can you die from this?"

Throughout, there has been a marked self-reference in L. B.'s attempts to understand death. Navarra tells us, without quoting details from his records, that these self-references gradually diminished "as the developing concept began to include information pertaining to withering, rotting, and decay."[12]

The second theme concerns the concept of gravity. Its interest lies in several features: first, that it even occurs, and in a very real and meaningful way; second, that it shows very dramatically the potent influence that a new word, introduced inadvertently, can exercise on a child's observations; third, that it shows how experiences and information that earlier had been quite unconnected with each other are suddenly subjected to reinterpretation and become related to a new theme. Navarra deals with this example under the heading *insurgent information*—that is, information that goes counter to everything the child knows from his past experience and interpretations and causes a kind of revolution in his vision of things. Here is the event that sets the chain of events going (Navarra unfortunately does not state the age of the child, but it appears to be when he is nearing 5 years):

L. B. had read to him a story about Christopher Columbus and the discovery of America. Much emphasis was placed on the fact that Columbus believed the earth was similar to a round ball in shape. L. B. listened quite intently during all the reading. At the completion of the story he commented: "You know, I think Columbus was wrong." When asked why he thought Columbus was wrong, L. B. replied: "Because on a round ball you could fall off—just like something flat." L. B.'s father said he wasn't quite sure what L. B. meant and L. B. carefully explained: "You know the round part? Well, you can take one step. But, that's all, *because* that's the end of the round ball." The adult said, "It seems that way, doesn't it?" L. B. nodded his head. "That's right, Daddy."

The adult did not tell the child wherein he was wrong. Rather,

some nine days later a small globe of the earth was given to L. B.
The various land surfaces were depicted in relief on the globe.
L. B. and his father used the globe to trace Columbus' voyage across
the Atlantic Ocean. Then India, Japan, and China were pointed
out as the original destinations of Columbus. L. B. became very
interested in the colors. L. B.'s father volunteered the names of the
various colored areas. L. B. recalled stories which he had heard
in connection with some of these places. Then, during the
discussion, he pointed to the bottom section of the globe, and very
deliberately inquired: "Do people live down here?" An affirmative
answer was followed by much spirited inquiry, during which
L. B. announced: "They would fall off." L. B.'s father attempted to
explain that the people were held to the earth by gravity. The
adult made some rather rash statements about "everything" being
"held to earth" by gravity. In a burst of enthusiasm, the father
even used wooden matches with one end stuck in modeling clay to
represent people standing all around the globe. L. B. listened very
patiently to all the father had to say and then very diplomatically
said, "Daddy, I *don't believe* in those stories about gravity." The
father, somewhat dismayed, asked, "Why not?" L. B. shook his
head: "Because an airplane can stay up and it doesn't fall down."
The father replied: "You're right, airplanes don't fall down; but
some other things do."[13]

However, although the child has rejected "gravity" as an explanation because it does not fit in with his observations, it is now a word
signifying something with which he feels compelled to come to terms.
He had suspected that his father was telling him a "story" ("I
don't believe in those *stories* about gravity"), and stories were not,
for him, credible sources of information about "real" things. (This,
incidentally, does not mean he disdained them; he loved them and
did not demand that a story reflect "real" things and events.) On
the other hand, it was his father who had told him this, and he could
not fail to notice that his father, after all, was serious and had not
been telling a story, in which anything could happen. And so we
find that L. B. engaged for a while in intense activity that was all in
some way related to his first confrontation with gravity as an explanation of why people do not drop into space from the South Pole.

His interest in toy and paper airplanes and in airplanes generally became very strong. Remember, his counterargument against what his father had told him about the power of gravity had been: "Because an airplane can stay up and it doesn't fall down." He had had this interest before, but now it became much more intense, and there is no doubt that he was relating his observations to the mystery of what is implied by gravity, for a little later the following incident is described:

L. B. recalled an animated cartoon he had seen via television: "Dad, I was looking at 'Junior Frolics' and Farmer Gray went up in a plane—the propeller fell off, and the plane came down." L. B. paused and then continued: "The moral to the story was: all things that go up must come down. Is that gravity, Daddy?" L. B.'s father agreed and added: "Once the motor stopped, the airplane was pulled back to earth by gravity."[14]

So now he gradually began to realize that the fact than an airplane can stay up is a special case that does not necessarily contradict the notion of gravity. He was now very interested in balloons and asked questions about them:

L. B. looked at an illustration of a man holding inflated balloons by a string, and inquired, "How can they stay up in the air like that?" His father attempted to avoid the question. "They're up in the air, aren't they? Don't you think they should be?" L. B. shook his head and said, "You know, Daddy, I had a balloon in a store and it went all the way up and I didn't throw it."[15]

"I didn't throw it": What does this imply? Simply that there is a dawning awareness of a thrust or counterforce to counteract the force of gravity, if objects like airplanes and balloons are to stay up and not fall to the ground.

Just as in the example of death, L. B. enacted the phenomenon in which he was interested with his own body. In that case he held himself stiff and tried to see how long he could stay "dead"; he now enacted the experience of gravity:

L. B. lifted one foot from the ground, precariously balanced himself by holding on to a chair and asked, "How can we pick up our feet when we walk?" Before an answer could come, he continued, "In quicksand, we can't, and gravity doesn't have anything to do

with quicksand—Ow, my leg. It's hard to hold it up. It felt like
it had to go down."[16]

L. B.'s dawning awareness of a counterforce to overcome the pull
of gravity was also evident from the attention he paid to the motors
of airplanes. At first motors seemed to be associated mainly with
noise; now he formulated their function:

L. B. had become entwined in the string attached to some balloons
with which he was playing. As he attempted to untangle himself,
L. B. inquired, "Mom, could this pull me up in the sky?" Mother
assured L. B. that the balloons would not carry him off. Then
L. B. described how Farmer Gray had been carried aloft in a huge
balloon. L. B. added, as he completed his description of Farmer
Gray's plight: ". . . and it didn't have a motor. How could it go up
without a motor?" Mother asked, "What good would a motor do?"
L. B. paused, and then replied, "Planes are iron but they could
fly because they have motors."[17]

The need for a counterforce is implied in more and more of his
questions that relate to things in which he had previously been interested for other reasons. He began specifically to mention wind:
"Does the wind hold up the balloon?" At first wind and air were
quite unconnected, and he defined the difference between the two
in terms of his own experience of strength: "Air isn't as strong as
wind. The air can't hold anything up." Gradually, however, he began
to understand wind as air in motion. And he began to ask questions
about many other things that he had seen before: "Mommy, how
can a bird stay up in the sky? . . . Can a bird stay up in the sky
without even flying? . . . What holds up a cloud? What holds the
moon up?" He asked new questions about these familiar phenomena,
and placed them in a new context, and more and more things seemed
suddenly to be relevant to each other.

L. B. turning the globe, pointed to the lower half and said, "Isn't it
funny, Mommy?—Their feet go down here (L. B. pointed to the
globe surface) and their heads go down here." After L. B. finished
speaking, he waved his hand through the air immediately below
the lower surface of the globe. Mother agreed: "Yes, gravity makes
that possible. It holds us up." L. B. interjected, "It doesn't hold us

up. It holds us down." He paused and then continued: "We pick
our feet up, but we can't pick them up long. . . . You know what?
A magnet can hold things up, and it can hold things down; and
if you put the magnet up, it holds things up."[18]

Here the record ends. Needless to say, L. B. had magnets among
his toys.

SPONTANEITY AND NONSPONTANEITY

Let us look at the term *spontaneous* now in the light of what we
know about L. B. His formation of concepts is spontaneous in the
sense that it is set in motion by actual confrontation with objects he
perceives and occurrences and actions in which he is involved.

Schachtel speaks of all children, except the most severely dis-
turbed, as going "through the childhood period of openness toward
and fascination with a yet unlabelled environment."[19] When, as
often happens, we say spontaneous formation of concepts is the
result of activity the child initiates himself, we are therefore stating
only a half-truth. The child does not initiate the activity—the activity
is initiated in him by phenomena whose fascination he cannot escape.
He does concentrate, it is true, to an extent that would make many
a schoolteacher envious, but he does this in response to fascination,
not as a result of acceptance of a task.

The introduction of language, or "labeling," as Schachtel calls
it, does not destroy the spontaneity of his concept formation. In the
period from age 3 to age 5, there was a great deal of labeling going
on, and L. B.'s vocabulary was particularly good. In the examples
quoted, certain words such as "fake," "real," and "gravity," which he
had obtained from people in his environment, had a terrific impact
on his further observations and their explanation and categorization;
his fascination with natural phenomena had remained strong because
of the way in which the words were introduced. "Language itself,"
says Schachtel, "like the parents, imparts certain viewpoints which
can . . . open or obscure the world."[20] L. B. was not given words
with the implication: This is all there is to know, this is as the adult
knows it to be; nor was he overwhelmed by words. He was given
leads that clearly implied that there is a great deal more to the

phenomenon and that it is by turning to the phenomena themselves that one can discover more. Words, as used in the sequences quoted by Navarra, are not merely labels that classify according to the accepted, conventional view of adults but pointers to the phenomena themselves and to relationships between them.

On the other hand, L. B.'s concept formation is not spontaneous in the sense that he would get as far as he does without the help of the adults who care for him. Openness to the world, and the exploration it leads to, we find only in children who feel reasonably secure and do not experience the world as a threat. But over and above this, even the completely secure child needs adults to respond to him and to give direction to his exploration. L. B.'s parents respond to him not only by listening, watching, and showing interest but also by helping him clarify his own observations, directing his attention to something, and providing him with new words that open up (rather than closing or settling) new possibilities of observation and explanation. The parents very effectively enter *his* world, but in doing so they bring perspectives from their own adult world.

Without this kind of response from his parents, and *in an environment in which causal and rational explanation do not permeate the thinking of the adults,* L. B. would probably still have been momentarily puzzled, excited, or frightened by natural phenomena. But it is not at all certain whether the *direction* of his interest—toward looking for explanations of natural phenomena *as* natural phenomena —and the *integration* of so much of his experience into themes, which we can recognize as the subject matter of science, would have been the same.

This doubt is reinforced when we look at the research of Basil Bernstein. Bernstein does not deal specifically with the child's conception of natural phenomena; however, in investigating the role of language in orienting children, he has shown how the child from the lower social classes in England is oriented by the language used between parents and children in a way that is quite different from the orientation of the typical middle-class child.[21]

Nevertheless, there must be many children whose confrontation with natural phenomena takes the same direction and leads to similar integrations of experience into the themes of science as in the case of L. B., for the interest in causal and rational explanation is widely diffused in our Western culture. In some cultures such causal and rational explanations play only a minor role—a point that will be discussed in the next chapter.

Topics for
Further Exploration

1.   In this chapter it was pointed out that the young child does a great deal of his learning in play situations. Observe some preschool children from an economically depressed area at play and then some children from a typical middle-class area at play. What are they learning? Are they learning the same things? Is there a difference in the verbalization during play, either in amount or in kind? If there are differences, how do you explain them?

2.   Read Jean Piaget's *The Child's Conception of the World* (New York: Humanities, reprint of 1929 ed.; Totowa, New Jersey: Littlefield, 1969, pb.). Then compare the picture of the child's conception of natural phenomena that emerges from Navarra's study with that which emerges in Piaget's book. Analyze possible reasons for the completely different findings with regard to anthropomorphic, animistic, magical, and phenomenistic explanations by young children. Is L. B. just an unusual child? Could the methodology—naturalistic setting as against an experimental one—have something to do with it?

3.   How does learning in school differ from the learning of L. B. in this study? Is it inevitable that there should be a marked difference between learning in school and the learning exhibited by L. B.?

References and Comments

1.   Ernest G. Schachtel, *Metamorphosis* (New York: Basic Books, 1959), p. 292.

2.   Note, e.g., what Susan Isaacs said in *Intellectual Growth in Young Children* (London: Routledge, 1930) in recording the experiences of young children at the Malting House school in 1924–1927. Her records indicate that the child's reaction to and observation of animals is much more likely to evoke responses and questions that lead to an interest in "scientific" biological explanations than his interest in flowers and flowering plants: "Flowers and flowering plants in the garden, as we know well, attract even the very young

child's attention by their bright colors and pleasant smells, and these remain a permanent source of interest and keen pleasure. The bright colors and varying shapes give rise to their use as *gifts* and as *decorations*, and these seem to be the most significant and spontaneous ways of regarding flowers which young children show. Occasionally the different forms or ways of growth evoke a mild interest for their own sakes, but this is fleeting and sporadic in these early years unless more or less compulsorily turned into a 'subject' by adults" (p. 168). As against this: "The observations . . . very strongly suggest (a) that children of the ages covered (4–10) are on the whole more actively and spontaneously interested in animals than in plants; (b) that the facts of the life-cycle in animals are far more easily and directly perceived and understood by the child; (c) that the interest in animals is far more genuinely biological, plants being often little more than gifts and decorations; and (d) that this interest is therefore more easily sustained and articulated, and ramifies more naturally into cumulative knowledge and settled pursuits" (pp. 159–160).

3. W. F. Leopold, *Speech Development of a Bilingual Child*, 4 vols. (New York: Bureau of Publications, Teachers College, Columbia University, 1939–1949).

   M. M. Lewis, *Infant Speech: A Study of the Beginnings of Language* (London: Kegan Paul, 1936).

   E. Scupin and G. Scupin, *Bubis erste Kindheit* (Leipzig: Grieben, 1907).

   E. Scupin and G. Scupin, *Bubi im vierten bis sechsten Lebensjahr* (Leipzig: Grieben, 1910).

   W. Stern and C. Stern, *Die Kindersprache* (Leipzig: Barth, 1928). Reprinted by Wissenschaftliche Buchesellschaft, Darmstadt, 1965.

4. John G. Navarra, *The Development of Scientific Concepts in a Young Child* (New York: Teachers College Press, 1955).

5. Ibid., p. 29.

6. Ibid., pp. 30–31.

7. Ibid., p. 93.

8. Ibid., p. 93.

9. Ibid., p. 94.

10. Ibid., p. 94.

11. Ibid., p. 96.

12. Ibid., p. 97.

13. Ibid., pp. 111–112.
14. Ibid., p. 117.
15. Ibid., p. 118.
16. Ibid., p. 118.
17. Ibid., p. 119.
18. Ibid., p. 120.
19. Schachtel, op. cit., p. 186.
20. Ibid., p. 186.
21. B. Bernstein, "Social Structure, Language, and Learning," *Educational Research* 3 (1961):163–176.

CHAPTER 6

Language, Cognition, and the Development of Intellectual Abilities

Thus, we may say that we become ourselves through others and that this rule applies not only to the personality as a whole, but also to the history of every individual function.[1]

L. S. Vygotsky

In Chapter 4 we tried to show that language and speech are involved in almost every aspect of human development: social, emotional, and cognitive. We gave some examples, too, to indicate that sentence structure and grammatical rules provide the speaker and the listener with distinctions about objects (e.g., some are countable, some are not) and events (they may be in the past, the present, or the future, etc.), and that the consideration of some of these relationships prompted Brown and Bellugi to say that a mother, in expanding a child's language and using the correct grammatical forms, may be teaching more than grammar—she may be teaching a "world-view." In Chapter 5 we illustrated how the speech of an adult, coming at an opportune moment in a young child's confrontation with natural phenomena, can reorient his further exploration and thinking. What we must do now is explore the relationship between language and cognition more fully and consider some of the ways in which the child's intellectual abilities are formed.

LANGUAGE AND THOUGHT

The discussion of the relationship between language and thought is a very old one in philosophy. What is included (and what is excluded) depends very much on the basic assumptions we make about the nature of thinking and language. If the criteria for thinking are taken from logic and concept formation in the modern natural sciences, the analysis of the role of language will tend to reveal the inadequacies of and pitfalls in natural language when used for these purposes. For example, Carnap investigates and classifies linguistically expressed judgments in order to arrive at a "logical syntax of scientific language,"[2] and modern formal logic introduces a formal symbolism in order to overcome the ambiguity of the grammatical forms and syntactical relationships of ordinary language. In using such an approach—which is perfectly justified for certain purposes of the logician and the natural scientist—we are narrowing our vision to see only one form of thinking and language in only one of its many aspects.

If we want to explore the relationship between language and thinking in a developmental-educational context, we cannot take our criteria for thinking from logic and concept formation in the natural sciences, nor can we look only at the function of language that manifests itself in highly abstract logical reasoning. Rather, we must see what is usually called thinking in the broader context of cognition in general, and we must look at the whole range of functions of language, not just those that serve the purpose of concept formation in any particular field of systematic thinking such as mathematics, physics, or biology.[3]

DEFINITION OF COGNITION

What do we mean by *cognition*? To cognize simply means to become aware of. We can, therefore, define cognition as any activity of becoming (or being) aware of something or having an object of consciousness. The "something" can be input emanating from outside my own body, such as a flash of light or a man walking, or input from various parts of my own body, such as my visceral organs. The overt

indication that there is awareness (cognition) may be a verbal statement (such as "I see the man walking" or "I don't feel very well
today"), or it may be simply a nonverbal behavior (such as focusing
the eyes on the man walking or physical restlessness and fidgeting).
In the course of everyday living, we formulate only a small part of
our cognitions, and the infant, before he can speak, also cognizes.

Our definition of cognition, then, does not confine itself to
"awareness of something" that is articulated in words and sentences.
It also includes simple organismic (bodily) responses to input. Also,
it does not confine itself to activities we usually call intellectual or
conceptual, such as categorizing, classifying, generalizing, and en-
gaging in deductive thinking. Rather, it includes also what we may
call affective or emotional awareness (to be discussed more fully later
in this chapter). What is suggested is that there is a continuum
ranging from bodily activity to articulation of cognitions in speech
and from vague affective awareness to highly conceptual activity in
dealing with knowledge. The definition given here can accommodate
traditional distinctions such as that between sensations, percepts, and
concepts, between enacting, ikonic representation, and symbolic
representation (Bruner), between sensorimotor, perceptual, and
symbolic activity (Werner and Kaplan), or between sensorimotor
activity, concrete operations, and formal operations (Piaget), but it
is broader than these distinctions imply. The notion that there is a
continuum along which cognitive activity has to be seen has two
important implications. In the context of trying to understand cognition in the adult, the notion of a continuum warns us against focusing too narrowly on just one segment of the continuum to the neglect
of, for instance, the relationship of affect to conceptualization. The
current interest in North America in "body language" and sensitivity
training could be interpreted as a reaction against the schools' and
universities' one-sided preoccupation with the symbolic and conceptual extreme of the continuum. In a developmental-educational context (which is our concern here), our task is to try to understand how
the child's cognitive activity moves from affective awareness and
direct bodily reactions to input toward symbolic and conceptual transformations and elaborations of that input. In terms of a distinction
made by Werner and Kaplan, the task for us is to understand how the

child moves from *reacting to* to *knowing about*.[4] The thrust toward "knowing about" may be, as Werner and Kaplan say, something typically human (monkeys show curiosity but do not build elaborate theories and discuss them), but it has its beginnings in organismic "reacting to" and maintains its roots there.

We have spoken of the two extremes of the continuum of cognition; what about what lies in between? Recall that we defined cognition as any activity of becoming aware of something or having an object of consciousness. An infant may indicate to us by his behavior that he is responding to something "out there," but this is only the beginning of the formation of a world of objects and the relationships between them. It is useful to think of cognition occurring at different levels of consciousness. Looking at the child from birth to, say, 3 years of age, examples of different levels might be: immediate organic reaction; more or less directed action (as distinguished from "reflex" or "automatic reaction"); action in a setting with other people where grasping may become pointing to something the other is to see, clearly implying that the infant has before him an object of cognition he wants to share with someone else; participation in a situation in which language plays a role; and active use of language so that language refers to at least some of the objects of cognition to which the child wants to draw attention, even though context and nonverbal cues may still have to carry the main burden of communicating about the objects. Each new level implies more processing of the initial sensory input.

Closely related to this concept of increasing reflectiveness is what we may call distantiating oneself from what one is experiencing. By this is meant that instead of being lost in organic sensation or at the mercy of strong emotions or under the compulsion to act and react only, in the course of normal growth the child becomes able to reflect on those experiences—that is, to look at them from a greater distance. Language is extremely important here. For instance, when the child can speak about his pain, his anger, or the events that have frightened him, the pain and the anger and the fright have been to some extent "objectified"; the child has greater distance from his own experience, and sharing the experience helps him set it in a wider perspective.

Cognition also occurs within different fields of experience and areas of concern. Let us take an example that is within the experience of every child. (We shall speak in the first person so as to bring home to the reader the infant's and child's experience more vividly.) Water may be what I drink when I am thirsty, and I enjoy it as something that refreshes me; I may move my legs through it or play with it merely because I enjoy the pleasant sensations aroused in me; I may discover that one should not go under it and I may develop fear or at least caution, and my experience informs me of an inherent quality of water that in another area of concern, such as quenching my thirst, I had not suspected; I may learn to use the water, combining it with sand and pebbles to make a mixture for a sand castle; I may learn to put the water into vessels for drinking, for pouring it out in play, or for carrying it from one place to another; I may learn to deal with it by learning to swim in it, thus incorporating water in ever-widening networks of my action. I can learn many other things about water; by observation, for instance, I can learn that animals like ducks live on or in it—animals that I discover I cannot catch, but I can feed— on the other hand, fish also live in the water and can be caught by bigger, more "grown-up" children, or I can feed fish in a fishbowl, etc.

Water, like any other "object" I experience and of which I became aware, is many-faceted, and the guise in which I learn to know about it reveals not only the inherent nature of water but also the dimensions of personal relevance that come into play as I "cognize" water.

THE DEVELOPMENT OF COGNITION

Cognition, then, *emerges out of and remains embedded in an inter-actional relationship*. Cognition starts with what at first may be only momentary arrests of attention by way of sensory inputs that signal possible significance for the organism; language is in no way involved yet.

We can illustrate this premise by looking at some extracts from biographies of babies. Joseph Church's book *Three Babies: Biographies of Cognitive Development* gives excellent data, and we shall quote a number of examples from it.[5] The newborn infant spends most of its time sleeping, but it also has periods of wakefulness, and within these periods of freedom from pressing urges and wants (food, elimination, etc.) it responds to outside stimulation and very soon even seeks such stimulation. In the biography of Debbie, one of the girls reported on in the book, the mother notes during the first week after birth: "After nursing, she does not sleep in my arms but seems content to be cuddled and rocked *while she peers up at my face*" (italics added). The French psychologist Guillaume reports, in connection with another child, that at 9 to 11 days he noticed an astonished and attentive expression directed toward faces, and fleeting smiles.[6] But it is not only visual input that may lead to momentary arrests of attention in babies; some sounds also may have a signal or cue character very early in life and may lead to selective acts of attention. The nurses' report about Debbie in the first week reads: "You're going to have some time with that one. She stops crying when she hears one of us walk through the door. She doesn't wait until she can see us at all." We read about Debbie in the second week: "Music turned on (radio) during these periods seems to please her, too. She notes its appearance by moving her eyes towards the source, and if it disappears seems restless for several minutes." Moreover, with regard to certain stimuli, her attention, even at this early age, is not even fleeting: "Follows familiar figures through doorways with her eyes and stares constantly at the door for their reappearance for up to ten minutes—is not distracted from this waiting by closer stimuli for long, and turns eyes and/or head back toward the doorway."

OBJECT CONSTANCY

All the examples quoted except one refer to the infant's cognition of significant people in its own life. There appears to be an important difference between the infant's cognition of such people and its cognition of things. A characteristic of people is that they come into the child's field of vision and hearing, and leave again. Moreover, people minister to the child's needs, turn toward the child, and stimulate it, and the infant learns to expect that people will come and go. The awareness that people continue to exist even when they are not visibly present comes very early, much earlier than the awareness that things like toys continue to exist when they are not graspable or within the field of vision. We find, for instance, the following entries concerning Ruth, another baby whose development is recorded in Church's book: "At nine weeks her head also turns to moving objects, but if they move out of her range of vision, she does not look for them. They seem no longer to exist." At the age of 5 months and 9 days, the following incident is mentioned: "If one takes away one of Ruth's toys, she looks at the place where it was and cries. She has no idea where it has gone. Nor does she look for it anywhere else." Only as late as the age of 9 months and 12 days are the indications clear that Ruth is aware of the continued existence of the toy that has been removed from her field of vision or her grasp: "Ruth remembers objects, even if they are out of sight. Whenever she sees a scrap of paper on the floor and I cover it with a book or my foot, she takes away the foot or my book and grabs the scrap. If I hide a toy behind a pillow, Ruth moves the pillow away. And she will not be distracted from her search." The diary of Debbie, which is less complete in its recording of such incidents, also reports incidents of this awareness at the age of 9 months and some days.

This phenomenon—that is, the awareness that an object continues to exist even when it cannot be perceived—is referred to in the literature as *object constancy*. Piaget has also observed it, and he attaches great importance to its emergence in the infant.[7] Schachtel makes an important comment on this phenomenon:

This observation implies not merely a purely intellectual development, namely of the idea of object constancy, but primarily it signifies a very important expansion of activity-affect. The child remains *interested* in the object, even though he can't see it. Activity-affect from this stage on can be felt not only in relation to perceived objects but also in relation to ideas of objects and of activities, and it is this felt aspect of the drive or interest which links child and adult to the world.[8]

In other words, affect, or feeling, is involved in building up a world of objects. If no feeling were attached to our ideas of objects and events, they would be "meaningless" to us. This is perhaps why so much of what is learned at school and crammed for examinations is seen as "irrelevant"—that is, as being without "meaning for me."

However, an object is not the same to the infant and the toddler as it is to the adult. An "object" is a result of experience and recurrence of experience. The same object—a toy, a chair, a table, etc., or for that matter, water—is experienced over and over again by the infant against a more or less stable background. In the course of such recurrent experiencing, the infant registers, as it were, "this one" as something separate from other "this ones," and he registers provisionally what "belongs together," to use the phrase of Erwin Straus.[9] Obviously language plays no role as yet. And equally obvious the object is certainly not yet a special instance of a particular class of objects.

In the world of the baby, objects or things *function* (that is, they function implicitly) either as part of oneself (for instance, clothes, bottle when in the baby's mouth, rattle when in the baby's hand) or as objects that are within reach *and* graspable. In other words, objects are related to the infant as a functioning center. However, objects become functionless when they are out of reach or are not connected with the acting or potentially acting self. For the infant there are objects, but only in a restricted sense of their existence. An object at first exists only as part of the infant's functional region or action space. Objects are, to the infant, what he can suck, touch, shake, pull, go to, climb up on, lick, bite, eat, cuddle up to, and so on.

The infant has an action space. This is necessarily very circumscribed at first; its limits and boundaries are determined by the means the infant has at its disposal for reaching out into his immediate environment. People and animals move and come into the field of action. If things do this, such as when an adult places a toy before the child and then hides it, they are threatening or funny. As the child becomes more mobile and more flexible in the use of his body, limbs, and eyes, the action space widens. But it is not only increased physical power, agility, and flexibility that widens the action space. The child learns that he can act upon things he does not see, things he cannot reach with its arms. He learns, for instance, to use a stick to extend his reach; he learns to point to things and by means of gestures and bodily movements indicate to adults what he wants and make adults do for him what he cannot do unaided. Much later he learns to call things by their names and generally, by means of language, to refer to things that are not present. In this way, more and more things can be incorporated into the action field of the child, and things that are not seen come to play an important part in the action field.

COGNITION AND AFFECT

The examples we have chosen of early cognitive activity illustrate yet another fundamental point about cognition in general that we are apt to forget when we look at the logical characteristics of thought rather than at the psychological processes of cognition: Whatever is cognized is something that in some way "affects" the infant closely and arouses *affect*, or emotion. We have already referred to this in our definition of cognition. The process of cognition is embedded in affect; an affective awareness (German: *Zumutesein*) is prior to full cognitive awareness. This view was expressed many years ago by F. Krueger in his theory of emotions,[10] and it appears in recent experimental work on the development of perception. The intensity of the sensory stimuli is less important than what they signify in terms of relevance to the infant's purposes and existing affective and cognitive awareness. Church gives the following example: "The young infant is oblivious to the screaming sirens of the fire trucks that go racketing past, to the hubbub of the thunderstorm, to the clamor of the doorbell or telephone, but he may wail in distress when his mother sneezes in the next room." From this he draws the conclusion: "Here we are saying two things: that the child perceives only personally meaningful objects, and that what he perceives is not so much objects as their meanings." In the terms we have been using, the child perceives only what is part of his functional field, or action space. Church goes on to point out that what is true for the perception of the child remains basic to perception in the adult too: "Developmentally and micro-genetically, meanings precede objects in perception. As Flavell and Draguns have noted, it is this principle that enables us to understand 'subliminal perception', *the fact that we can react affectively to something without being able to identify the something to which we are reacting*" (italics added).[11]

Cognition, including the increasing objectification and elaboration by language of what has been perceived or experienced, never loses its rootedness in affect and in the action field of the child. It is simply that as the cognitive horizon widens and becomes more differentiated, the person changes too, and as the person changes, phenomena that previously had no significance for him become relevant. Having and building up a cognitive world also implies being and forming a personality; as the cognitive horizon widens, the child must somehow interpret and cope with the increased complexity.

Whatever "getting to know" there is in the very young infant is predominantly nonreflective and in the service of his most basic needs. One hesitates almost to use the term *cognition* here—the reaction to stimuli is often so direct, and there is so little deliberation. And yet there is a link between the earliest selective reactions to sensory input and the later feats of deliberate representation and symbolic thought that transform the sensory input and delay the time between stimulation and action.[12] Debbie's relatively prolonged peering at the face of her mother is not an act of representation and symbolic thought but an act of attention (though preconceptual) that leads inevitably to increasing differentiation between "the other" and "the I." Very soon there will be not only rapt absorption but pleased *re*-cognition, evidenced by the smile: In the third week "Debbie very definitely smiles at familiar faces—and more fully so if these faces smile at her."

The acts of re-cognizing, having a world of familiar people, things, and recurring events, build up a world in which one can anticipate. For as new impressions stream in as the child interacts with an ever-widening world of people and things, a base and an anchorage are provided for this learning, this growth, by the already familiar people and things and recurring events in his world. Many new cognitions occur against the background of what is already part of the expected—that is, the preconceptual order of the familiar world. Although many other new cognitions are at first unrelated, they provide foci for further cognitions. Novelty, and incongruities between previous cognitions and present ones, may cause anything from wonderment to fear to pleasant surprise. The stranger smiling at Debbie in her third week produced "only a serious stare." When at the age of 5 months Benjamin (the third child in Church's book) sees his father's face covered with shaving cream, he "looked at him hard and then his lower lip thrust out and he would have burst into tears if I hadn't carted him off downstairs." On the other hand, a little earlier in Benjamin's life: "Several times he has become aware of Sam (the dog) and once of another dog, and has laughed and laughed. . . ."

SCHEMATIZATION

All in all, long *before language plays any role in the child's own cognition*, the infant gets to know the world as a place where many regularities occur. A term that is often used to describe the infant's experiencing of these predictable regularities is *schematization*.[13] Church defines a *schema* as follows: "Psychologically, the schema has two faces. On the environmental side, we become sensitive to regularities in the way things are constituted and act, so that we perceive the environment as coherent and orderly, in ways that the adult can make explicit as principles but that, for the baby, exist only in the sense that here is the world and things are under pretty good control. On the organismic side, schemata exist in our mobilizations to act and react, which in turn reflect the environmental properties to which we are sensitive."[14]

Schematization is not something characteristically human. Harlow's experimental studies of monkeys and chimpanzees "learning to learn" as well as of sensory deprivation in various animal species seem to show this.[15] Harlow speaks of the acquisition of *learning sets*, but when we look closely at what is involved here, it appears to be very much the same as what is described in the acquisition of schemas: that is, sensitivity to how things are arranged and mobilization to react to them in certain ways. After a sufficient number of trials, a monkey learns to *expect* a grape under a cup of a certain color or shape, regardless of its position; that is, the animal becomes sensitive to the regularity that has been built into the experimental situation. When a new, more complex, "abstract" regularity is introduced (for instance, the grape is now regularly under a cup of a different color, regardles of which colors are used—i.e., the "oddity" problem), the monkey eventually discovers this regularity too. Once a learning set has been acquired, it is retained. Animals that have already acquired simple learning sets are quicker at acquiring the more complex ones than those that have not yet acquired the most elementary learning sets. Moreover, the different learning sets do not seem to interfere with each other; they function as relatively separate units, and the organism becomes flexible in switching from one to another.

However, *what* is schematized, what the regularities are to which the human infant becomes directed and sensitized, will be very different for the infant, for his schematization of experience is in an environment that is structured and interpreted by human beings. We return, therefore, to the point we have often made in previous chapters: The human child does not begin his life as an isolated organism but in a close, almost symbiotic relationship with his mother. He is not alone in his interaction with the world. He not merely perceives and cognizes but does so in cooperation and interaction with his mother. What is cognized will depend not only on the needs of the organism qua organism and the selective filtering of sensory input by the reticular activating system[16] but also on the alerting of the infant by the mother and on what one might call the *coresponsive participation* of mother and child in a common world.

CORESPONSITIVITY

In this coresponsive participation, where sometimes the infant takes the lead and sometimes the mother (or other adult), the infant's cognitions are constantly supported, reinforced, and brought into relationship with those of the participating adult. Moreover, while every mother knows perfectly well that the infant cannot understand a word of what she speaks, she speaks to the child nevertheless and catches, directs, or holds his attention with speech. Debbie may be an exceptional child of exceptional parents, but even if the following example had been recorded for a child of 3 to 4 months instead of 1 month and 8 days, it would still illustrate the point that the child starts very early to respond differentially to the stream of language directed at it: "She invariably responds to being called by name by turning to the source of the call (visible or not) and by a look of suspenseful but pleasurable waiting attentiveness. This response is specific to the words 'Debbie' and 'LooLee.' She pays no particular attention to other words called out in the same voice unless they resemble phonetically the two noted above (such as 'every' or 'NooNee')." Speech sounds themselves, as well as the whole of the speech activity, become objects of cognition for the infant. The speech directed toward the child also elicits an impulse to utter sounds, or "speak." Debbie, at age 2 to 3 months, increasingly vocal, "engaged in answering-type conversations with both parents lasting four or five minutes, total body straining prominent as she tries to vary the tonal range, or make various lingual and labial sounds." Ruth is also stimulated by the adults to vocalize: "Ruth makes cooing noises, but only when she is being played with and spoken to, and on these occasions only when she is comfortable and happy, and very engrossed in the person playing with her. . . . First she has to be totally engrossed in the person talking to her, then she smiles, then she strains her mouth, head, and body, opens her mouth soundlessly several times, and then, finally coos."[17] And Benjamin, at the age of 2 to 3 months: "Yesterday he was lying in the cot in his room well-fed, and I was bending over him. He smiled several times, very gaily, and I began saying hi to him, over and over, opening my mouth quite wide each time. *I'm sure he started to imitate me.* He kept opening his mouth and once or twice made a little sound as if trying to imitate the sound also"; a little later: "He 'talks' . . . He smiles a great deal—almost laughs sometimes, and is *most* responsive to talk and to singing."[18]

The speech of the adult, then, elicits "speech" in the child, although by no means necessarily the same sounds and much less the same "words." Although what the child utters is not language, communicative intent and intention to speak *about* something seems to enter the speech activity very early.

The mother, sharing in the infant's delight at the appearance of a pet dog or his startle at an unfamiliar sight, does more than just react to the stimuli in the same way as the infant; she looks at what the child is pointing to or points herself, or she may playfully imitate the action that has excited the interest of the child or imitate the response of the child itself, or both; and she will almost certainly speak to the child too. But even if she did not speak, there is enough in her coresponsive behavior to make it clear that the direct chain of stimulus and response is being broken, and an element of representation (of both stimulus and response) is being introduced. A great deal has been written about the baby's imitation of the adult; the role of the adult's imitation of the baby in furthering the child's own efforts toward representation and symbolization appears to be equally important. A child that is encouraged to reenact something just experienced by seeing the parent reenact it is beginning to take events out of the stream of experience and "objectify." "Look," he seems to be saying, without speaking a word, "this is what I have just experienced." The ground is being prepared for acts of referring to an experience not by partial reenactments but by the symbolic means of language.

It will be useful now to summarize briefly what we have said about the nature of early cognition:

1. Some stimuli have *signal* or *cue* character because they are significant in terms of the infant's purposes at an almost completely nonreflective organismic level.

2. Emotional significance, or meaning in terms of threat and promise to the perceiver, is prior to the perception of an object *as* object.

3. In the interaction between the infant and the world in which he lives, the infant becomes sensitive to regularities and builds up expectancies (schemas, learning sets).

4. Coresponsive participation by adult and child in a common world increasingly encourages the infant to point to and in a rudimentary way "re-present" and thus "symbolize" events that in the beginning appear to have only signal or cue character; there is beginning to appear some distantiation between the child's direct experience of an event and the self, which "objectifies" the event.

5. In the first year the representing and "symbolizing" is not yet done by means of conventional symbols of language, but speech has become an object of cognition (the infant begins to be sensitive to some regularities in the speech of the adult, as shown by his responses to some utterances), and as an activity speech is becoming

more and more interlocked with cognition and with communication of what is cognized. As Church puts it in *Language and the Discovery of Reality*: "The child is not learning merely to speak, or to understand words, or to build up a stock of words—he is learning a whole mode of behavior, the linguistic, *which is prior to any particular symbolic acts in which he may engage*" (italics added).[19]

We come now to consider what happens when the child has acquired the symbolic mode and both his vocabulary and his syntax begin to improve at the rapid rate we mentioned earlier. What is the relationship between language and cognition now?

THE SYMBOLIC MODE AND COGNITION

We begin by noting that when the child has acquired the symbolic mode of language, the direct involvement of the child with his world is still of utmost importance to his cognitive development. He goes on building up schemas and expectancies—becoming sensitive to regularities and mobilized toward experiencing and dealing with them. What is experienced in the transactional process between organism and environment, the person and his world, is never emotionally neutral but frightens or excites or amuses or puzzles or delights, and invites to action or manipulation or avoidance or—and this is new, once the symbolic mode has been acquired—symbolic rendering. It is not as though language can suddenly—at age 2 or 4 or 6 or 11 or even 60—make redundant the person's direct involvement with the world that presents itself to his senses, invites or rejects his approach, yields or resists his manipulation, dominates or serves his purposes, and thus forces itself into his affective and cognitive awareness. Language is not a deus ex machina that solves all the problems of getting to know, of rubricating and categorizing what the individual child ought to know in the opinion of the adults involved or according to the prescriptions of the culture. Language is not a substitute for direct experience (although in pathological cases it can almost become this); it is itself a mode of experiencing and an activity of apprehending and transforming direct experience as well as symbolically mediated experience.

Language creates new channels through which the mother (and other people) reach the child and orient his activity and cognition; it also enables the child to do new things for himself and to do old things more efficiently.

SPEECH AS REGULATING BEHAVIOR

Controlling and directing the child's behavior is an aspect of early language development that has been stressed by many psychologists (such as Lewis) and especially by Russian psychologists (such as Luria).[20] "No, no" may at first be no more than an acoustic signal, a stimulus to which the child is conditioned, but a remarkable thing soon happens: He produces the signal himself and inhibits his own actions by telling himself "No"—for example, when he is about to grab the flower pot, an action for which he has been sternly admonished with "No," a great deal of fuss, and perhaps a slap on the hand. The "No" doesn't remain for long only the particular *mobilization to desist* ("Don't touch the flower pot") implanted by the adult. It can be turned to many uses: to resist the inhibition the adult tries to impose or to resist the lines of action demanded by the adult and assert his independence ("No!" when told to go to bed; "No, no" when offered help), as a statement of fact or a counter-assertion ("No, I'm not hungry"; "No, mine is bigger"). A simple word used by an adult to inhibit an action of a child carries within it the seeds of many meanings, which are re-created by the child in the process of using it in ever-new contexts of ongoing experience. Ruth, at the age of 10 months, "cannot say no, but she shakes her head in refusal"; at the age of 15 to 16½ months: "She walks around saying 'No-no' or 'Not' (Do not touch) and shaking her finger at all the objects she may not touch. She enjoys this game—perhaps because of my approval, perhaps because she is proud of herself for remembering. She says 'No' in a scolding voice (like mine?) and she does this when I am near." Only one or two months later, at age 17 or 18 months, there is already considerable variety in her use of "No": "Her 'No' is sometimes serious, sometimes means 'yes', sometimes is a show of independence, and sometimes is whimsical."

Apparently "No" is used by the child earlier than "Yes," though one case is recorded in which they seem to have been acquired simultaneously and remarkably early.[21]

However, controlling and directing behavior through language involves not just "No" and "Yes"; it involves an increasing range of words as well as increasingly complex sentence constructions: "Don't do *this*, do *that*"; "Don't look here, you silly, look *there*"; "Take the *spoon*, not the *hand*"; "When you have finished eating, you can play again." Now, the striking thing is that, just as the child begins suddenly to utter "No" as part of the process of inhibiting an impulse or changing the direction of an activity, so he begins also to accompany his actions with all sorts of other utterances that have a bearing on the activity in which he is engaged: "not here—there—take the spoon—good," etc. Just as the adult has regulated the child's actions with verbal descriptions and directives, so the child now seems to do it himself. And because so much of what the child does as an accompaniment to his activity seems to involve mapping and planning that activity, formulating what the obstacles and intentions are, and evaluating the outcome, speech here seems to have the characteristics of "thought." It is this phenomenon that leads Vygotsky to say that typically *human* thinking arises from the adult's regulation of the child's behavior by means of language and that the social or communicative and thinking or cognitive functions of language are at first quite undifferentiated.[22]

INHIBITED, EGOCENTRIC, AND INNER SPEECH

Vygotsky's views (available to us in the English translation of papers written before 1936 but published under the title *Language and Thought* only in 1962) are so fundamental to the present-day discussion of the relationship between language and the development of intellectual abilities that a few comments are in order. Vygotsky formulated his conception of the origin of typically human thinking in an attempt to come to grips with two theories that had just been propounded by psychologists when he wrote: the theory of the founder of behaviorism, Watson, according to which thinking is nothing but "inhibited speech," and that of Piaget, developed early in his career, according to which the child's language up to the age of about 6 years is predominantly "egocentric" and not genuinely communicative or social in intent.[23]

As one piece of evidence to support his view, Watson had given the observation that in the development of speech the child at first only speaks aloud and cannot inhibit his speech in order to whisper, but gradually he learns to whisper (in kindergarten and the lower classes of elementary school, however, he may at times still find it difficult—he has to speak aloud when confronted with a difficult problem). Watson projected this process further: Later the whisper develops into inaudible speech—that is, into hardly measurable impulses towards speech, the existence of which Watson tried to "prove" experimentally by apparatus to record laryngeal movements. Since all we can observe is the activity of speaking (straining of body, laryngeal movement) and since, according to the tenet of Watson's extreme behaviorism, only what is "observable" can be said to exist, only speech exists, and what we "unscientifically" label *thought* is "really" speech, whether this speech-thinking is audible or not.

Vygotsky concedes the observable facts and commends Watson's search for a link between the "overt" speech of the young child and the later "inner" speech. However, he believes there are other observable facts that have to be taken into account: First, before the infant starts speaking he is also "thinking"—if we include, as we must, problem solving at a perceptual and manipulative level as evidence of a form of thinking;[24] second, and more crucial, the functions of speech and the structure of speech utterances were not taken into account by Watson—he was too preoccupied with the dimension of audibility.

Piaget, on the other hand, is very much concerned with the function of speech. According to Vygotsky, however, Piaget misinterprets the function of speech and pays insufficient attention to the syntactic structure of speech utterances.

Piaget's observation on preschool children showed that they made statements in each other's presence rather than to each other, not really checking whether the other was listening or not, understanding or not—each child, so to speak, orbiting in his own world, blissfully unaware of the fact that, in order to communicate with the other, adjustments to the other's "point of view" are required. Language at first, according to Piaget, is not social but "egocentric."[25]

It is only as the child gains more and more experience with peers (Piaget has to this day emphasized the importance of peers rather than adults for the cognitive development of the child) that *misunderstandings and conflicts* gradually force on him the realization that a point of view is relative to the perceiver or the actor; language thus becomes "socialized" and more communicative in intent. Corresponding to egocentric language, there is egocentric thought.

According to Vygotsky, the speaking aloud to oneself that Piaget sees merely as a reflection of an egocentric orientation toward reality has a function he has overlooked and at the same time is more dependent on social interaction than Piaget was led to believe. Vygotsky reports experiments with young children engaged in activities like drawing. The records of the language used indicate that it reflects the planning and mapping out of operations and intentions. When the examiner creates an obstacle (e.g., removes a required or desired crayon color beforehand, the level of verbalization rises: "Where's the pencil? I need a blue pencil. Never mind, I'll draw with the red one and wet it with water, it will become dark and look like blue."[26] There is more verbalizing when there is another child present, even though the language used all refers to the planning and evaluating of the activity; clearly, the awareness of the other's presence stimulates speech activity.

Finally, the structure of the statements is revealing. The utterances a 3-year-old makes when he obviously wants to communicate something to someone else are not very different from those he makes when "thinking aloud" in connection with an activity in which he is engaged. In both cases it is abbreviated language: Sentences are not fully formed, one word may stand for a whole sentence, the subject may be omitted, etc. This in itself is nothing remarkable, since it has always been noted that children normally start speaking with short utterances, not full-fledged sentences in which a thought is properly articulated. The person addressed or the person observing can only understand the child's utterances if he knows the total context of the action and is in close rapport with the child (as the mother normally is). Speech and action are still closely fused— speech is still *synpraxic*; that is, it can only be understood in the context of the action within which it is embedded.

As the child's linguistic competence increases, the structure of the utterances in both situations (communicating or thinking aloud) becomes more complex. But then a differentiation sets in: What is said with communicative intent becomes more and more articulated, or put into full sentences; the speaking aloud as planning, mapping, or evaluating becomes more and more abbreviated, until finally speaking aloud becomes the exception rather than the rule. But though the older child or adolescent or adult no longer speaks aloud to himself all the time when engaged in a project (i.e., when "thinking"), a process of silent formulation goes on most of the time. Overt speech has become inner speech.[27]

Vygotsky believes the silent formulations of inner speech are also abbreviated. Abbreviation is thus a characteristic of synpraxic speech, of speaking aloud as a form of thinking (what, according to Vygotsky, Piaget had interpreted too exclusively as reflecting an ego-centric orientation of the child toward reality) as well as inner speech involved in thinking. Synpraxic speech, which is inevitable at the beginning of child development because the child is not yet capable of articulating his experience in sufficiently differentiated utterances (sentences, accurate grammar), is also found in many situations in which older children, adolescents, or adults engage in a common activity: They can afford to utter just a single word and still be understood because the total situation—the context—supplies the rest of the sentence.

Where either audible or silent formulation carries forward the process of thinking or problem solving, abbreviation is possible because the thinker is, as it were, his own audience and is formulating against a background of ongoing experience that he does not have to make explicit to the outside observer.

However, Vygotsky's concept of *inner speech* should not be confused with Watson's *inhibited speech*. When Vygotsky speaks of inner speech, he is not thinking in the first place of the criteria of audibility or inaudibility, or of the activity of the speech organs. He is thinking primarily of semantic and syntactic criteria. When he speaks of inner speech as *speech*, he is thinking of the process of formulation in language, even if the words flit across "consciousness" only and involve no demonstrable activity of the speech organs whatsoever. Moreover, while for Watson thinking was "nothing but" inhibited speech, Vygotsky never really discards the distinction between thinking and speech but believes the process of thinking becomes inextricably interwoven with (mostly silent) formulations in terms of language. Inner speech is not thought; it is a constituent of the process of thinking. The latter, however, can never be the same again once language has entered into it. The flexibility of thinking is enhanced; it becomes differentiated and objectified; the history of human experience enters into it; it becomes communicable.

The soliloquies of the 2½-year-old Anthony in *Language in the Crib*, of which Ruth Weir says that they are really dialogues in which speaker and listener are combined in the same person, would also support Vygotsky's notion of the origin of typically human thinking in an originally social situation (see also Chapter 4). The well-known phenomenon of a child indulging in make-believe and playing different roles, creating a whole dialogue in the process, would be in line with Vygotsky's theory too. This last phenomenon has its parallel in the "make-believe" of the adult who clarifies his experience or intentions or insights by formulating to himself, silently, what the participants in a discussion said or what different people *would* say about it. Imaginative writing in all its forms is another manifestation of the same tendencies at work. Thought, it seems, not only has its origins in a social situation in which the adult first "regulates" the behavior of the child by means of speech but also requires the experiencing of alternative possibilities.

The view that, in using inner speech to carry forward the process of thinking, language is abbreviated has often been questioned. Roger Brown has argued that it is virtually impossible to prove or disprove this assertion.[28] The truth is probably that it sometimes is and sometimes is not. A single word may be enough for us to get a first grip on an experience or argument or idea, and in the course of a long process of thinking many such links may be left vague. However, anyone who has ever written a paper or addressed an audience knows that in the process of writing the paper or preparing the address in detail he does far more than just make his thoughts communicable; he is developing his thoughts and may on occasion be astonished to find how different the fully articulated thought is from what he believed it to be before he had gone to the trouble of formulating it in full sentences and sequences of sentences. The student who thinks he knows something discovers to his distress that he does not "really" know it when he has to write down his thoughts on that topic for the examiner. The lecturer discovers the gaps in his reasoning as the lecturing situation forces on him the need to make his thoughts explicit. The language we use in communication and the one we use in thinking is, after all, the same language. It is not *either* a means of communication *or* an instrument of thought; it is both at the same time. The language we use in communicating our thought to others does not find a thought that already exists in its final and unalterable form but articulates the thought and may change it in the process. In formulating something, we sometimes discover what we "really" think. Nor do we as adults always think in solitude and in silence: We seek partners for discussion for the purpose of clarifying our thought. And when we write a book we need an editor to fill in the occasional gaps or straighten out the sometimes tortured reasoning.

We do not know how Vygotsky would have developed some of the ideas that are merely implicit in his account of the relationship between language and thought, but it is worth pointing up some of the important aspects of this relationship about which he has said little or nothing.

EGOCENTRIC SPEECH AND EDUCATION

While Vygotsky has drawn attention to the fact that the structuring of the relatively brief *experimental* situation in which children are observed (e.g., introducing obstacles to their activity) affects the nature and function of the language used, he has said little or nothing about the more enduring and embracing socioeducational situations in which the acting and feeling and speaking and thinking of the child are embedded. The fairly numerous replications of Piaget's work on "egocentric" speech,[29] which have usually produced results different from Piaget's, have also missed this point. These studies are, in fact, too little concerned with adequate theory that might explain the divergent findings and too prone to attribute the divergencies to differences in the populations from which the children were drawn (without, however, giving an analysis of the *psychologically significant* socioeducational characteristics of those populations) or to methodological factors.

In the ninth edition of a book that is seldom cited in the North American literature, William Stern has given a brilliant analysis of the effect on experimental findings of the socioeducational matrix within which the child has his experiences and learns to speak and think.[30] Stern points out that the children observed by Piaget in Geneva were in a Montessori-type kindergarten. He then quotes the results of an investigation by Muchow in a Fröbel-type kindergarten in Hamburg, where a replication of Piaget's investigation produced a much lower proportion of "egocentric" speech. Stern argues very plausibly that the differences in results are due to the very different structuring, not of the experimental conditions under which the children were observed (these were comparable) but of the socioeducational situations in the two types of institutions. The traditional, orthodox Montessori-type kindergarten treats the children as individualists, each engaged in his own activities with the "materials" (blocks, cylinders, beads, containers, etc.) that are supposed to enrich his sensory experience and on the basis of which certain concepts are to "develop."

The Fröbel-type kindergarten, by contrast, emphasizes socioeducational experience within small groups, including children of different ages and an adult, a situation in which much more dialogue is encouraged and other people (particularly the older and more experienced ones) are sources of information to which one can turn. Stern points out that this dialogue becomes even more marked when we look at the normal situation in the educated home, where the child carries on his activities within the family circle—that is, with adults who have time for the child and with older and younger siblings. He quotes a study by Katz and Katz,[31] who collected samples of young children's language as used in family situations: Here language is used *preponderantly* to get information and to give information, ask questions and make counterassertions, follow up what the other has said, and share experience. Thoughts are developed in a dialogue; Stern uses the term *Sprechdenken* (i.e., "speech-thought") to characterize the samples of language provided by Katz and Katz.

THEMATIZATION

It is necessary to point out that when analyzing speaking aloud as a process of "mapping" or "planning," Vygotsky is speaking rather exclusively of problem solving in a concrete, practical situation. The use of language for this purpose is undoubtedly important. When the toddler is becoming more and more mobile, he explores his immediate environment and in the course of this indulges in much "problem solving" at a perceptual-practical level; here language does seem to play the role Vygotsky suggests. Bruner calls this "representation in symbols *for* action."[32] There is here a kind of extension of the schematization of the prelinguistic period, except that language now helps stabilize the schemas, thus getting them under control. Also, in the direct interaction with the environment schemas will go on being formed, and linguistic formulation will continue to play its role in stabilizing them.

But, concurrent with this activity, something else is happening that calls for coping with experience of a different kind, and even to the 3-, 4-, and 5-year-old this becomes overwhelmingly important. The adult not only regulates the activity of the child in the sense already indicated but shows him pictures, tells him stories, and tells him about animals, people, countries, and events the child can only imagine. Radio and television bring him information and experience that he would never have if left merely to explore his immediate, nonsymbolic, "physical" environment, even if he learned to use language to map and plan his activities. Thus, while the child soon gets to know his immediate environment in the sense that he can move about in it and in some way manipulate it, symbolically mediated experience is streaming in at a very fast rate indeed; it changes his experience of what is perceptually given and directly manipulable by bringing it into juxtaposition with what exists in the realm of "once upon a time" and "in the future" and "in other places," and in realms of reality, imagination, and possibility that intersect and shift and weave a multidimensional network revealing ever-new depths and interconnections. If he is not to be overwhelmed, he must relate his experiences to each other, and in fact the child does try to build up a coherent world of meaning.

Of course, the adult may notice mainly the unconnectedness of much of the child's knowledge and experience, and the seeming lack of logic in the way different items and levels of experience are related to each other. But what is remarkable is that the child connects experiences that may lie far apart in time and information that comes from very different sources around areas of personal concern that we can call *themes*. Navarra's study of scientific concept formation in a young child, which we have described and interpreted, shows us the nature of themes of a particular kind; we saw how the activity of the child himself, the sources of information, the help and encouragement of the parents, and the language made available to the child (language acting as a "lure for cognition," to use Roger Brown's phrase) all contributed to the emergence of the theme and to the incorporation of more and more experience into coherent themes that resolved cognitive conflict, created expectations into which new experience could fit, and created new cognitive conflicts. We saw, too, that themes relating to what the adult in our society categorizes as natural science have repercussions for the child's awareness of himself.

The child thematizes his experience. The formation of *themes* and the formation of *schemas*, described earlier, should not be confused: The themes presuppose the schemas. Thematization is something more than using language to carry forward thinking of the problem-solving type in an ongoing practical activity. And the themes do not involve only explanations of natural phenomena. They also involve the interpretation of interpersonal behavior, including that which the child experiences directly within his family or circle of friends as well as that which is symbolically mediated in stories, fairy tales, and puppet theatres, and on television. In addition, his own likes and dislikes, expectations and frustrations, conduct regarded as good or bad, desirable or undesirable, and his emerging self-concept are involved.

Far too little is known about the effect of interpersonal experiences on cognition. A change in sibling position when a new baby arrives may involve, as is well known, feelings of jealousy, rivalry, and rejection. Certainly feelings are involved, but in coping with his feelings the child is helped not only by the reassurance he gets through the attention paid him but also by a process of conceptualizing and formulating his feelings and his situation. Merleau-Ponty[33] quotes a case study by Francois Rostand, who recorded the new language acquisitions that accompanied a 2- to 3-year-old child's shift from being the youngest in the family (two children) to being the middle child (when a baby was born). At the birth of the baby, the 3-year-old's language first regressed along with his other behavior. But then he began to formulate his changed relation to his older brother as a result of the birth of the baby, and he became aware of the process of change in which he was caught up—of a past dimension and a future dimension. In language he now began to use the simple past tense, the imperfect ("I was going"), the simple future tense, and the future tense with the verb "to go," and he used these to formulate the *change* from his former condition ("I was small") to his present one ("I am not the smallest") and to the anticipated future condition ("I am going to be big"). In this case is the interpersonal experience as a result of the birth of a baby related to the new time distinctions the child is making, or is it just coincidental? We do not know.

We need far more detailed and varied records of such observations to be able to assess their validity and to see the growth of themes and their coalescence into broader and more inclusive ones. Psychotherapists are very much aware of the fact that the function of language is not simply to designate and deal with a "reality" that is "external" to us but rather to bring to light our experience of that alleged reality and our as-yet-unnamed feelings, evaluations of impulses, and attitudes.[34] Developmental psychologists know of its importance, too, but have very little empirical data to offer. No doubt this is due partly to the fact that the emergence and growth of a theme over a number of days or even years cannot be studied in the laboratory, but it is probably due also to a prevailing tendency to regard feelings as less worthy objects of attention for the cognitive psychologist than the abstractions of mathematics and physics that support our technological civilization.[35]

But cognition, we must repeat, is any act of cognizing. Objectifying and clarifying, by naming and formulating more precisely our individual feelings, impulses, and motives, is as important to individual development as learning to understand the concept of gravity in physics or that of homeostasis in biology. Developmentally, articulating our feelings, motives, and intentions verbally may even be basic to the sustained achievement of concepts in the field of science, for apart from clarifying and suitably modifying, where necessary, the child's own concept of himself and his purposes, and his relationships to others, articulation in language orients the child toward ways of perceiving abstract relationships that are important to abstract "scientific" thinking, too.

If, as we said earlier, "cognizing" is indicated by any "momentary arrest of attention," what happens *after* the first momentary arrest of attention is important. That which arrested the attention (something impinging on the sensory apparatus, such as actions, impulses, emotions, or feelings) can either fall back into an unanalyzed stream of experience, of unreflecting response to stimuli and signals, or it can become *objectified*.[36] Objectifying implies changing an experience into an "object" of attention, taking it out of the flow of experience and thereby changing our emotional relationship to it, or putting it into a category and into a set of relationships.

This last point is worth developing more fully, and we can turn to Bernstein's analysis of the function and characteristics of the language used in different social classes in order to do so.[37]

SOCIAL CLASS AND LANGUAGE

The comparison of the characteristics of the language utterances of children and adults in the lower- and middle-class English groups that Bernstein studied can be summarized very briefly by the labels he uses: One is a *restricted code*, the other an *elaborated code*. The oft-noted paucity of the uneducated or lower-class child's vocabulary Bernstein regards as far less significant than his inability to exploit the *formal possibilities of language* as given by syntax, grammatical distinctions, and the use of functors (see Chapter 4). The lower-class child's language tends to consist of short sentences, which are often incomplete or amorphous. His statements do not "spell out" the whole situation to which they refer but take a great deal of context for granted; thus, he is easily misunderstood by a person not thoroughly familiar with the context in which he is speaking. His language is abbreviated and retains the characteristics of synpraxic language. For emphasis he is likely to indulge in gesturing and/or repetition instead of varying the phrases in order to specify his meaning more closely. Words indicating relationships tend to be used loosely or not at all. The possibilities inherent in the English language with regard to time distinctions (tenses) are not exploited very fully, either.

The characteristics of language used are, of course, related to the function of speech, and it is the analysis of this function that makes Bernstein's work particularly relevant to the point we are trying to make about the importance for cognitive development of using language to clarify feelings and motives.

For the lower-class child the function of language is to reinforce group values, not to ask "Why?" The language used by the mother in interaction with her child carries within it no challenge to look for causes, effects, or wider implications and does not encourage the child to make fine distinctions; it directs the concrete behavior of the child in the concrete situation and does not distinguish between action and motive or between the specific instance and the general case. The middle-class mother also reinforces group values and behavior acceptable to the group (and if necessary she will be just as effective in *enforcing* a particular kind of behavior), but the middle-class mother's values include emphasis on understanding the reasons for and consequences of acts as well as on individual responsibility and achievement. Two samples of language quoted by Bernstein can best illustrate the contrast. A mother has her little child sitting on her lap in a bus.

I.   Lower class

> Mother: Hold on tight.
> Child: Why?
> Mother: Hold on tight!
> Child: Why?
> Mother: You'll fall.
> Child: Why?
> Mother: I told you to hold on tight, didn't I?

II. Middle class

> Mother: Hold on tightly, darling.
> Child: Why?
> Mother: If you don't you will be thrown forward and you'll fall.
> Child: Why?
> Mother: Because if the bus suddenly stops you'll jerk forward onto the seat in front.
> Child: Why?
> Mother: Now darling, hold on tightly and don't make such a fuss!

It is clear that the restricted code, which the lower-class mother is using, is entirely adequate for enforcing a particular kind of behavior in a particular situation. On the other hand, the elaborated code, which the middle-class mother is using, goes beyond enforcement of specific behavior in a specific situation: The statement "If . . . (then) you will . . ." analyzes the whole situation in terms of cause and effect, and further contains a model or an analogue for analyzing other situations in such terms.

The language used in punishing and reprimanding children shows similar contrasts. The middle-class child is made much more aware of motives as distinct from actions and of the reasons why one act is punishable and the other not. The very fact that his individual motives are taken into account and verbalized places emphasis on acts not only in the context of group requirements but also in the context of highly personalized individual experience. Punishment is seldom so direct and quick as in the lower-class family,[38] but the very act of speaking and being spoken to about the behavior enables the child to assess his own behavior in terms of his motives, its effects on others, and his own emerging code. The child learns to relate his impulses and desires to the objective requirements that he himself is prepared to accept.

One 4-year-old from a middle-class family was overheard saying, not with bitterness or protest but with full acceptance of the objective requirements as being reasonable: "I don't want to, but I must."

This was not a case of potentially disruptive repression of instinctual impulses but of the growth-promoting subordination of momentary wishes to an objective order of things that has become meaningful and "binding" to the child. Just as "If . . . (then) you will . . ." lifts the special instance out of its concreteness and uniqueness, and gives an analogue for cause-and-effect thinking, so the statement "I don't want to, but I must" implies the description not of a single experience only but of a whole class of experiences in which impulse and requirement have to be weighed against each other. The 4-year-old will meet many such experiences. It is an analogue for bringing impulse under control. For all the directness of punishment and conformity to group values in the children of lower classes, it is the acts that are brought under control rather than the impulses. Bernstein speaks of impulsiveness and nonreflectiveness as characteristic of lower-class children. The individuation as well as generalization of experience in terms of language seem to play a significant role in promoting both reflectiveness and impulse control.

Now, Bernstein is interested in the relationship between the function and structure of language in the early years of the child's development and the growth of the intellectual abilities that are relevant to success at school. In fact, it is the attempt to understand the divergent patterns of scholastic achievement between middle-class and lower-class children that leads him to analyze the function and structure of language in different social settings. With regard to the scholastic attainment of the lower-class children, he finds a characteristic pattern: They are likely to have some difficulty in learning to read and in language work; their interest is aroused by novelty, but it is difficult to interest them for long in following up implications of what they are observing or experiencing. Nevertheless, for the first 5 or 6 years at school their measured scholastic performance may not be so markedly lower (if at all) than that of their middle-class counterparts. However, when after the first few years the school begins to demand a much more abstract, "symbolic" approach, they tend to lose all interest and are out of their depth. In passing, it should be mentioned that this pattern is well known from studies in many parts of the world of groups of either "low class" or "low socioeconomic status" or "culturally deviant and poor" groups who are exposed to modern Western-type schooling.[39]

Bernstein believes, and argues very plausibly, that the real barrier to learning at school for the lower-class child lies in the fact that his experience has not provided him, early and consistently, with ways of specifying, differentiating, and generalizing personal experience or even with the desire to do so. The "elaborate code" the school tries to teach is largely meaningless to him because he does not appreciate or value its function. This does not mean teachers can do nothing about it, but they will not get very far unless they aim to make language *function in a new way* in the lives of these children. Cause-and-effect thinking; interest in implications that have to be imagined and hypothesized, and require symbolic rendering; the abstract relational thinking required in mathematics and science—the first steps toward these may have their origin in the elucidation and transformation of highly personal experience (actions, motives, feelings) in language. The examples Bernstein quotes have nothing to do directly with early number experiences or explanations of natural phenomena, yet they have implications for the latter.

RATIONAL COGNITION

Being sensitized to necessary and possible implications of one's acts through early experience and its linguistic articulation creates awareness of the ability to find rational explanations for events. A whole attitude toward knowledge and "getting to know" is shaped. If we want a label for this, we can call it *rational cognition*, a cognition that is ultimately concerned with establishing what relationships and causes and consequences are *inherent* in phenomena. It is this that makes possible what we have come to value so highly in Western European culture since the Renaissance—that is, "science," scientific attitudes, and the technology we can derive from the exploitation of scientific insights as well as from scientific ways of thinking.

As participants in this modern, post-Renaissance Western European culture, with its strong emphasis on the authority of reason rather than that of tradition, we are inclined to believe thought "naturally" tends toward rationality and logic.[40] The study of the cognitive development of children was, naturally enough, at first a study of children growing up in *our* society, and we have had an almost irresistible compulsion to generalize what we find in our culture to the development of children everywhere. We early "dis-covered" the fact of individual differences in intellectual ability and rates of development, and we conveniently tended at first to ascribe these much more to genetic endowment than to environmental factors. The work of sociologists like Bernstein shows us that even within the same culture the cognitive development of children in certain social subgroups may, by the preschool years, not take the direction we have come to regard as normal and inevitable, and that, whether or not genetic endowment plays a role,[41] the direction cognitive development takes is strongly dependent on the ways of perceiving and thinking and symbolically elaborating that are induced and encouraged in the child by the parents and by the pressure of his social group.

Language is important here—not language in isolation but lan-guage as it permeates and transforms the experience of the child and the whole fabric of socially oriented and socially embedded living. When we come to the study of children growing up in radically different cultures from our own, we become aware even more of how little we can take for granted about the "inevitability" of a certain course and direction of cognitive development and how necessary it is to be aware of cultural and educational factors that condition and give direction to the course of cognitive development. We turn to such studies now.

CULTURE AND COGNITION

By a radically different culture we usually mean what for want of a better word (and perhaps out of arrogance) we call a "primitive" culture. Social anthropologists have studied many such cultures for a long time and have given many accounts of how children grow up in such societies. Students of *cognitive* development in children, however, have only recently begun to exploit this literature sys-tematically and to conduct their own inquiries among children in "primitive" societies. The quickening interest in such studies co-incides with the spread of Western-type schooling to, and in, so-called underdeveloped (or "developing") countries. It is in this situation—a school with aims, purposes, modes of intellectual inquiry, and a whole way of life developed in one culture and now required to function in another—that we are jolted into reflecting on the cognitive orientations and abilities induced by the traditional culture and those the modern school needs and tries to create. Bruner dealt with some of the issues on his 1965 presidential address to the American Psychological Association;[42] so have Gay and Cole,[43] Olson,[44] Ramphal,[45] Schmidt,[46] and Schmidt and Nzimande,[47] among others. Such reflection has far-reaching consequences for our conception of human development and of cognitive development in particular.

We take as an example of such a study that by Gay and Cole: *The New Mathematics and an Old Culture: A Study of Learning Among the Kpelle of Liberia.* Although the inquiry centers on the teaching of mathematics, the authors find it necessary to analyze (1) the Kpelle language, in order to see what terms it makes available for denoting numerical and mathematical relationships, geometrical figures, groupings, sets, etc.; and, more significantly, (2) they also find it necessary to determine the basic orientation to "knowledge" (the meaning of "to know") of the adults as well as the children in that culture. In order to do so, they are compelled to try to understand the whole way of life of the people and the values and purposes implicit in their traditional education.

As regards the linguistic terms for geometrical shapes, we quote from Gay and Cole:

The most striking fact is the relative paucity of terms naming abstract geometric shapes. We have an abundance of such terms in English, that are used relatively often; there is apparently little need for them in Kpelle, and they are rarely used.[48]

They then give words for "line, straight line," "circle," "triangle," "quadrilateral," and some solids. We have put these terms in quotation marks to indicate what will become evident from our further quotations: that the so-called equivalents may not be true equivalents at all. We read, for example, that the term *pere*, path, can refer to a straight line. However, it can be applied equally well to a curved or jagged line. These distinctions, which we require in English are unimportant to the Kpelle. The important thing about that which they term *pere* is that it extends from one place to another without crossing itself.[49]

The last sentence should not be taken to imply that a Kpelle adult who has not studied mathematics in a Western-type school would define the word in this way; he would simply give examples of *pere* that lead the investigators, the products of a culture and education in which a certain kind of abstraction is encouraged and developed, to abstract and verbalize the common features contained in the examples. We continue quoting information about the term *pere*:

Interviews with informants showed that the term *pere* could be applied equally well to a straight row of stones and a meandering row of stones . . . when some informants were asked to organize a set of stones into patterns, the results were invariably irregular and unsymmetrical. Kpelle towns have no regular plan or order, except the social groupings by kinship. Houses are clustered in irregular and uncoordinated ways. There are no rows of more than three houses even in a large town, and the few rows of three seem fortuitous. When crops such as rice and cassava are planted, the rows are crooked. Only rubber farms planted by wealthy, Westernized people use the straight row pattern so familiar to Western culture.[50]

About the circle, we read:

The figure called *kere-kere*, "circle," does not have the precision of our word circle. It is the shape of a pot, a pan, a frog, a sledge hammer, a tortoise, a water turtle, and a rice fanner. Some of these are non-circular ellipses, and others may be irregularly closed shapes. The informants were aware of the difference and called the elliptical figure *koya*, "long," but the term *kere-kere* was still applicable. It is, therefore, close to our topological concept of a simple closed path, although some measure of circularity is required for the term to be used.[51]

The equivalent term for "triangle" is described as follows:

There is a term for triangle, *kpeilaa*. Some things to which this word is applied are a tortoise shell, an arrow head, a monkey's elbow, a drum shaped something like an hourglass, a bird's nest, and a bow. The term is not restricted to figures formed of three line segments, but includes other similar shapes.[52]

Finally, the quadrilateral:

By contrast, the term for quadrilaterial refers directly to the fact that the figure has four sides. It is called *bela-naan*, "four parts." Informants told us that a rectangular house, a plank, a doorway, a chair, and a table are all of this shape. All of these items have assumed a rectangular form only in modern times and it is possible that the term *bela-naan* has recently been coined by the Kpelle people.[53]

We omit Gay and Cole's references to terms for solids because these do not change the picture the examples quoted give us. There are two points we should note: (1) There is a paucity of terms for abstract geometrical shapes and (2) with the exception of the word for "quadrilateral," which according to Gay and Cole appears to be a recent addition in response to innovations in building materials and furniture, the word as it is used by the Kpelle adult still bears all the traces of its close link with *object-dominated and/or action-dominated perceptual experience*. Objects have properties that one knows from handling and using and seeing them, and among these properties there are figural ones. "A pot, a pan, a frog, a sledge hammer, a tortoise, a water turtle, and a rice fanner": All of these are experienced as having a similar shape for which the language has a name, *kere-kere* ("circle"). The language draws attention to a common or similar feature of "shape," but in order to speak about it, it is necessary to refer to objects. The question: "What *is* a circle?" or "What *is* a triangle?" is answered by quoting examples of familiar objects that share the characteristics of being "circular" or "triangular." The *concept* of a circle or triangle, completely abstracted from the objects, with properties about which one can reflect within a whole symbolic system of mathematics, is entirely missing.

We have not yet mentioned the linguistic system; in particular, we have said nothing about the functors, or *form words*, which are important in assessing the difficulties the Kpelle might have with certain logical reasoning processes. The following quotation summarizes Gay and Cole's findings in this regard:

They find disjunction easiest; in order of increasing difficulty are conjunction, negation, and implication. Equivalence they find very difficult. This pattern contrasts very significantly with American behavior, and many of the differences seem to reflect differences in linguistic structure between Kpelle and English.[54]

Now, how is the paucity of terms and the close linking of the meaning of the terms to action- and object-dominated perception likely to affect the cognitive development of the children growing up in this culture?

With regard to the first point, the paucity of terms simply reflects, as Gay and Cole themselves point out, that in the ordinary life of the Kpelle there is no need for further distinctions.

With regard to the second point, we have to remind ourselves that in our culture, too, the meanings attributed by the child to the words for abstract geometrical forms *his* language (English, German, French, etc.) makes available to him will at first also be object- and action-dominated. This, after all, is the way in which words are acquired: in the context of a transactional relationship with the world in which the child moves, acts, is acted upon, experiences objects in relation to himself, and experiences himself in relation to objects. The naming of "figural" characteristics that he experiences is in this respect no different from the naming of other "events" that, by the act of naming, are singled out and taken out of the flux of ongoing experiences. When the child has said "circle," he has not formed the concept of a circle, just as little as his first use of the word "ass" signifies that he has formed the concept of an ass: "a quadruped, *Equus asinus*, allied to the horse, but of smaller size, with long ears and a tufted tail." The *concept* of "circle" requires *logical* abstraction; the *naming* of the figural characteristic requires *psychological* abstraction.[55]

CONCEPT ATTAINMENT AND FORMATION

We ought at this stage to refer to the distinction often made between concept attainment and concept formation. Concept *attainment* refers to the acquisition and proper understanding of concepts that are already available in the language and thinking of the adults and are presented to the child to be "learned." Concept *formation* refers to the formation of entirely new concepts. Children are said to be concerned mainly with concept attainment—getting to know the concepts that have already been formed by others—i.e., the culturally available concepts. It is in some ways a very dangerous distinction to make, because it may easily prevent us from recognizing the active, creative role of the child in acquiring already available, preformed concepts. Nevertheless, it is a distinction that points up the dependence of the child's cognitive development on what is culturally available.

In modern Western society it is the school that systematically confronts the child with the concepts he is to acquire. But before the child comes to school, and outside school, he is in interaction with adults who, however much they may have forgotten the particular concepts they learned at school, have nevertheless acquired the modes of abstract concept formation that school taught them and at the very least know the existence of and have some familiarity with abstract symbolic systems such as that of mathematics or science. The Kpelle child, outside the Western-type school he attends, is in interaction with adults who not only have not acquired the particular mathematical or scientific concepts but also have not acquired the *modes of abstract concept formation* the Western-type school teaches.

In addition, if the modes of abstract concept formation do not have self-evident functional value outside the school—that is, within the matrix of social and economic activity of adults and the purposes and aims of the people that constitute a particular society—or require attitudes toward knowledge that run counter to traditional attitudes and thus may be experienced as threatening the stability of society, then the modes of thinking acquired at school may function in only very specialized contexts and may not "take root" properly.

About the Kpelle attitude toward knowledge, Gay and Cole write:

Important men in the village became angry when asked how they knew certain mathematical facts. They would not answer. This was not information to be given out lightly, even if they knew the answer. For the old people, a fact is a fact. It cannot be called into doubt. It is self-validating, and *needs no reason to support it.* The child who asks "why?" is considered "frisky" and is beaten for his curiosity [italics added].[56]

The second principal feature of the Kpelle pattern of education is that reasons need not be given for what is learned. *The fact that the activity performed and the secrets described are traditional is reason enough* [italics added].[57]

. . . The innovator, the man who might be able to do a particular task better than his predecessors, is frowned upon; independence is stifled, particularly within those areas where tradition is strong. That an individual or family be kept alive and healthy is not as important as maintaining the complex of customs that is the Kpelle way of life.[58]

However:

It is true that *in areas confined to specialists,* pragmatic use of intelligence is acceptable. For instance, innovation is allowed in carving and weaving; the blacksmith can vary his designs; doctors may find new medicinal secrets. *But the ordinary man* is expected to follow the traditional path, thus obeying the elders and, through them, continuing the history of the tribe. It should be noted that the variations permitted these specialists *in no way affect the traditional rhythm of life* [italics added].[59]

The Kpelle have all the words for knowing, believing, thinking, etc., but:

Knowledge is the ability to demonstrate one's mastery of the Kpelle way of life. Truth is the conformity of one's statements and actions to that way of life. . . . Those children who go to school and acquire a new set of values and ideals are simply regarded as tribal emigrants. They have joined a new tribe by their own choice [italics added].[60]

The examples quoted show that the Kpelle child, except during the time he is in the Western-type school, is expected to have attitudes toward knowledge that run directly counter to what the Western-type school takes for granted as being "natural": He is *not* expected to ask for rational or logical reasons or for cause and effect, not even with regard to pragmatic activities, but to find out and accept "what the elders say."

NEW KNOWLEDGE AS A THREAT

It would be misleading, of course, to assume that in Western society people never feel threatened by the knowledge and ways of thinking they acquire at school and by new knowledge and new ways of thinking and perceiving. We remind ourselves of what we described earlier as a basic characteristic of cognition even of the small infant: Whatever is cognized "affects" us and arouses affect or emotion, and we have to add now, with regard to the further development of cognition, that there are times when new knowledge and new ways of thinking may throw us into turmoil, threatening our whole relationship to reality and undermining the feeling of security that comes from being embedded in customary, familiar, shared ways of feeling and perceiving and behaving.[61]

What Galileo saw through his telescope threatened a whole way of life and aroused acute anxiety. The introduction of physics and chemistry into high school curricula was resisted for a long time, and what Theodor Litt writes of nineteenth-century attitudes toward these studies probably comes closest to the really underlying cause of the resistance to their introduction into the education of pupils at high school: It was the whole abstract and impersonal way of looking at reality that made people "shudder."[62]

But we need not turn only to the canvas of history to make our point. Scattered about in the European literature on the learning process (seen in an educational and developmental context and therefore not concerned merely with the learning of single tasks, as most of learning theory has been in the past), we find emphasis on the crisis-provoking impact of new knowledge. One thinks of Copei's "fruitful moment" in the process of education[63] or the concept of *exemplarisches Lernen* (i.e., in a somewhat crude translation that does not do justice to the multifaceted meaning contained in the original term, "proto-typical learning"), which recognizes the superior power of some kinds of knowledge as against others to reorientate the person cognitively.[64] For long stretches of time, learning may seem to consist mainly of a mosaic-like addition of new bits of knowledge, but at some point, usually unpredictable because we cannot see and may not even sense the subterranean threat to the child's naively assumed certainties, the child may suddenly become excited about a new item of knowledge or a generalization or principle, and he becomes personally and emotionally involved. He has to restructure all he knows and come to terms with its implications for himself, his beliefs, and his relationships to other people. There is attraction as well as threat in such new knowledge. The art of teaching, according to this view, consists of preparing the ground for "fruitful moments" to occur and then recognizing them and capitalizing on them: helping the child face the implications of the new knowledge. Festinger's work on *cognitive dissonance*[65] and the ideas of the neobehavioristic Berlyne on the relationship between curiosity and *epistemic behavior* on the one hand and anxiety on the other[66] could be cited in support of the view that knowledge is often experienced as threatening.

Nor should we be blind to the fact that in Western societies, too, children are not constantly or even exclusively expected and encouraged to ask for rational explanations rather than "what the elders say." To a considerable extent a child simply learns the customs, the traditional ways of behaving: what "we" do, how "we" do it, what "we" believe, what "we" want, what "we" ought to do. And this is learned by our children, too, through direct participation in the life of the group—by doing, and not asking awkward questions.

Nevertheless, there is a vast difference between the traditional education of the Kpelle and the education Western societies provide. At the pinnacle of the formalized educational system in Western societies, there is an institution that exists for the purpose of asking awkward questions: the university. While it is educationally necessary to protect children against drowning in vast seas of uncertainty, we conceive of the adult citizen as one who not only knows "what the elders say" but also questions the mores and asks for the reason "why." Books on child psychology, written for parents, are full of advice on the question: "How do I answer my child's question?" Teachers are exhorted to teach children to "think," not to memorize or to be satisfied with ideas only vaguely understood. By contrast, the *whole* of the traditional education of the Kpelle emphasizes participation and not what the Western-type school also, and characteristically, emphasizes: reflectiveness, verbalization, and abstraction.

Traditionally, the Kpelle also have a school: the "Bush school." Gay and Cole write:

At some point in his growth, the child enters Bush school. He may enter at age five, when he has barely begun to grow into the tradition. Or he may enter at any age up to about fifteen, when he would have been exposed to almost the entirety of the traditional

way of life. *His education in Bush school is not in any sense
a radical break in his pattern of growth; it simply intensifies* and
deepens what is already happening in all aspects of his life
[italics added].[67]

Gay and Cole's description of the actual method of teaching and
learning is similar in its essential features with what other writers
have said about other Bush schools; the children learn by participating, watching, and imitating:[68]

The life of the child "behind the fence" is largely a replica of his
life in the village, except that he sees no members of the opposite
sex. The adults and the children build a village in the forest,
make farms, hunt, and engage in all the daily activities of
village life. . . .[69]

THE SCHOOL AND SYMBOLIZATION

In Western society, on the other hand, the school prepares its young
for future participation as adult members of society partially by
direct participation during childhood but to a very large extent by
introducing him to highly abstract symbolic systems. The facts that
educational reformers introduce activity methods, project methods,
and the like in order to make learning more "real" or "natural" or
"spontaneous," or to improve "motivation for learning" and that
these methods can be employed very successfully in Western-type
schools (and possibly ought to be employed more) do not contradict
what we have just said: For even when these methods are used,
knowledge as we conceive it is knowledge at a high level of conceptualization and symbolization, available out of the context of
actual, concrete, ongoing activity. A completely different level of
reflectiveness and abstraction is intended, even if it is not always
attained. But the intention itself, the struggle to meet the demands
of a school that has this intention, pushes and pulls the cognitive
development in a direction that for human development is only one
of the possible ones, not the only naturally given and inevitable one.

We ought not to be surprised, then, to find that many modes of
thinking—categorizing, inferring, abstracting, grouping and ordering
arrays of information—that we associate with a certain age of a child

and use as an index of the intelligence or cognitive level attained by the child may in fact be heavily dependent on Western-type schooling.[70]

STAGES OF COGNITIVE DEVELOPMENT: DUE TO WESTERN SCHOOLING?

According to one very prominent school of thought, the *sequence* of cognitive development is everywhere the same, but the different stages may be reached at earlier or later ages, depending on "cultural" and "environmental" or even "educational" factors. This is the school of thought represented by Piaget. It should be noted that, contrary to what many critics have said about Piaget, cultural and environmental and educational factors are taken into account in this view, but they are regarded merely as (slightly) facilitating or (slightly) retarding factors that affect the speed or rate at which cognitive development takes place, not its nature or direction. It is a grandiose, ethnocentric conception that regards the post-Renaissance ways of thinking of Western man, and more particularly the mathematical-physical-scientific modes of apprehending and interpreting reality, as the self-evident norm for cognitive development. It elevates one possibility of human nature into the grand design, the secret intent, of biologically given human nature.[71]

It seems much more likely that without the specific contribution of the Western-type school, with its heavy emphasis on reflectiveness and abstraction, and its meshing of the cognitive activity of the child into the symbolic systems that have been created and developed in the West (or taken over and appropriated from other cultures such as the Arabic), the whole direction of the children's cognitive development would be different. It would be a miracle if, without the stimulus of the Western-type school, the Kpelle child, for instance, rose to levels of abstraction and symbolization characteristic of the person educated in the Western tradition; it would be an even greater miracle if he "spontaneously" adopted the groupings and categorizations characteristic of such a person's thinking. Some empirical evidence for this point of view already exists, and a search of the anthropological literature would no doubt reveal much more.

Gay and Cole report on an experiment in classification—forming sets of objects according to different attributes. The task was a very simple one for children who have grown up in the Western tradition, and indeed the authors state that they had feared it would be far too simple for their Kpelle subjects too. There were eight cards, on which were pictured triangles and squares either red or green in color and either two or five in number. The task was to sort the cards into groups with common attributes—the attributes being, of course, color, number, or form. This is what Gay and Cole report:

The initial results were astonishing. The task was almost impossibly difficult for all three groups—illiterate children, school children, and adults. . . . We asked ourselves if the instructions were inadequate or the material on the cards too difficult to grasp. . . . First of all, we tried to make sure that the subjects understood the instructions by preparing a set of sample cards on which figures were drawn in ink. . . . The experimenter began by saying that this pack of cards could be sorted into two groups in different ways and then proceeded to form the groups in each of the three possible ways. The subject was then shown the pack of experimental cards and asked to perform the same kind of tasks. . . . Another possible factor was the cultural relevance of the cards. For this purpose we prepared eight cards identical to those described earlier, but using instead pictures of a woman beating rice, with a baby on her back, and a man carrying a bucket of water on his head, followed by a dog. These pictures were readily understood and accepted as culturally appropriate. There were either two or five pictures on a card. The cards themselves were either red or green. Thus, the cards could be sorted according to the picture (man-woman), color, and number. As before the subjects were requested to sort the cards in three different ways.[72]

The overall result is summarized as follows:

The overall effect of the demonstration sorting procedure was to increase the number of sorts that the people made. But severe problems remained. There were no significant differences between the ability to sort the triangle-square and the ability to sort the man-woman cards. . . . The most striking aspects of these data (given in a table, that is) are the relatively small proportion of subjects who managed even a second sort of the cards and the great amount of time each sort required. *The average American twelve-year-old takes one look at these cards and instantly proceeds to sort them into the three possible sets. The average Kpelle adult could not complete this task and only two-thirds of the Kpelle adults could make a second grouping.* Moreover, the amount of time for the sorts, from one or two minutes, is extraordinarily great [italics added].[73]

We cannot, of course, be sure whether the Kpelle child could not perform this task with relative ease if it were embedded in an activity in which it was important for him to be able to group items according to the attributes of color, form, or number, for in contrast to his failure on this task (and the average American's excellent perform-ance), the Kpelle can estimate the number of cups of rice in a large bowl remarkably accurately (whereas the American cannot). The truth of the matter is, however, that the Kpelle, even the adults, find the abstraction of such attributes as color, form, and number, *out of context* of meaningful ongoing activity (such as might be involved in buying articles in a shop), exceedingly difficult.

That the Western-type school plays a role in determining what kinds of classificatory behavior are likely to develop in children be-comes evident in a study by Schmidt and Nzimande, who carried out an investigation into color/form preference and classificatory behavior among both schooled and unschooled rural Zulu children.[74] For the unschooled children (ages 5 to 13 years), color was overwhelmingly the first basis for sorting in the tasks given (one of which was the same as that used by Gay and Cole), regardless of the age of the children. Again regardless of age, hardly any unschooled children were able to shift over to another basis for sorting (shape, number) when asked to find another way of sorting the cards. The children who were attending school showed a different pattern: The 5-year-olds at school gave the same responses as the children not at school, but after that there was a gradual shift from color to form preference, and with increasing age the children were able to switch to additional criteria for sorting.

The studies by Bruner and associates published under the title *Studies in Cognitive Growth* are part of a dialogue between Bruner and Piaget.[75] The book is dedicated to Piaget on his seventieth birthday, and it makes use of a great deal of Piaget's terminology, but at the same time it presents experimental data that contradict Piagetian hypotheses and theoretical discussion that is highly critical of Piaget. For the purposes of our argument, we do not need to become involved with the whole complexity of the alternative theoretical position Bruner is trying to formulate: his distinction between three forms of representation (enactive, ikonic, symbolic) and their interaction in the development of the child or his concern with relating man's growth to evolutionary history. We pick just one theme—the difference in performance between children and adults who have not attended a Western-type school and children who have, with respect to specific aspects of cognitive performance on well-known Piagetian tasks.

One of the coauthors of the book, Patricia Greenfield, describes an experimental investigation of *conservation of quantity* among the Wolof in Senegal. The basic experiment is as follows: A subject is presented with two beakers and asked to pour exactly the same amount of colored water into each. He is then told to pour the water from one of the beakers into a third, differently shaped beaker (narrower and higher or broader and lower) and asked whether this beaker contains the same amount of water or not. If the third beaker is thinner and the water level has risen, children under a certain age will often say that there is more water now; conversely, if the beaker is broader, they are inclined to say that there is now less water. Other beakers are used and the same question asked. When the child answers the question correctly and consistently, and no longer becomes confused by the appearance of inequality, he is said to have achieved conservation of quantity. According to Piaget the shift from nonconservation to conservation is something that comes not suddenly (e.g., as a result of being taught) but gradually, over a period of years, and is part of a wider, more embracing shift from what he calls "preoperational thinking" to "concrete operational thinking."[76]

Greenfield tested both rural and urban (Dakar) schoolchildren and rural unschooled children. All the schooled children of ages 11 to 13 years had achieved conservation of quantity, whereas barely 50 percent of the unschooled children had done so. Moreover, whereas

the difference in the number of schooled children achieving conservation at 6 to 7 years and those achieving it at 11 to 13 years is
very large, the difference in the number of unschooled children
achieving it at these two age levels is small. The gap between unschooled and schooled children *from the same village* is greater than
the gap between rural and urban schoolchildren.

This result would still fit in with Piaget's notion that environmental influences (including school as simply part of the environment) would affect the rate of cognitive development. However, the
following result no longer fits, for it indicates that, far from "out-
growing" perception-boundness (which the schooled child is able
to overcome), the unschooled Wolof children seem to increase their
dependence on perception: The latter give more perceptual reasons
for justifying their answers (that the water is now "more" or "less")
as they grow older and not fewer; this is in marked contrast to the
schooled children, who start off at 6 to 7 years giving mainly perceptual reasons and end up at 11 to 13 years giving very few.

In this connection Greenfield makes an important comment:

. . . One type of perceptual reason expresses a conflict between the
appearance ("It looks like more") and the reality ("But it's really
the same") of the situation. This type of reason occurred in the
conservation responses of American children . . . but did not
manifest itself in the African protocols. If any conflict between the
"appearance" and the "reality" of the situation exists for these
African children, it is expressed in different ways. In fact, previous
pilot work at the Institut d'Etudes Pédagogiques at the University
of Dakar had indicated that *there is no conventional way of
translating into Wolof the question oriented towards an appearance-
reality conflict*—"Is the water in the second glass 'really' different
or does it 'just look' different?"—*and that when the translation is
made the children do not understand what it means*
[italics added].[77]

This comment is especially striking when we place it next to what
Theodor Litt, to whom we have already referred, also said regarding
the resistance to the introduction of the physical sciences into the
education of children: People could not accept what they felt to be
the depreciation of naive, spontaneous, direct perception and the

elevation of the "scientific," abstract, mathematicized view of nature into the "true" reality.[78] That the sun does not "really" set bothers few of us today, for we have become accustomed to distinguishing between a prescientific (but not therefore unscientific) world of direct experiencing in which the warm glow of a *perceived* beautiful sunset is not depreciated by the scientifically derived knowledge concerning the shape of the earth, its rotation around its own axis, and the mathematically expressed laws of gravity. It does not bother us that when the physicist uses his sense perception he does it for the purpose of relating what he perceives (with or without the aid of instruments that amplify and specialize his perceptive powers) to an abstract theoretical system in which the "event" perceived confirms or refutes a hypothesis. We—and this means our children too—are exposed all the time to hypotheses that "make sense" only within the abstract symbolic system of science.

What does this imply for conservation of quantity by children? The *concept* of a *quantity* (of water, clay, cake, beads, books, or anything else) is, in fact, something no one can "see" in any literal sense. Water may change, may be "the same" or "different" in many ways. It may become dirty or clear, cold or warm; it may be in a glass with a shape that invites one to drink from it or in a flat beaker that obviously does not have this "appeal" quality. One has "more" or "less" of something, but the "more" or "less" is at first not a measure of quantity conceived in terms of a concept of quantity per se—that is, as part of a mathematical or physical system of ordering reality; it is, rather, quantity in terms of my directly experienced, prescientific desire for "more" or "less" of whatever it is (milk, cake, play, stories, going for a walk, etc.) in which I am involved. Quantity is first experienced in the prescientific, phenomenal world, in which a thin, long piece of clay, for example, is a "stick" and the same piece of clay rolled into a round, fat piece is a "ball"—and the two are obviously not "the same."[79]

To be able to grasp that a quantity of clay or of water remains "the same" despite changes in its direct appeal to the perceiving and acting person, the child must be oriented toward an abstract, symbolic system in which transformations of what is phenomenally perceived are no longer in conflict with the invariances abstracted in terms of the symbolic system. The symbolic system, of course, does not give us the "true" reality but reality at a different level and in one of its perspectives.[80] The spontaneous experience of the child lays the basis for this; the planned, structured experience the adults may provide in our society, even outside school, strengthens this foundation simply because they themselves think in terms of that system and it impinges on daily activities all the time. And finally, the Western-type school, through its structuring of experience for the child (always an important aspect of the total process of teaching and educating) as well as by means of straight teaching and telling, focuses the attention on quantity and measurement and number, and the whole network of concepts of the symbolic system that no one can "see" except in terms of a derived meaning of "see." As with the acquisition of language, the child himself discovers and re-creates (although not without considerable help) the symbolic system that already exists and thus learns to confront the prescientific, phenomenally experienced world with the "scientific," symbolically ordered reality and to be at home in both.[81]

In a society in which this symbolic system has not been formed or has not yet achieved a strong functional value within the matrix of the society's activities and purposes, the spontaneous experience of the child will also begin to lay a foundation for the concept formation that could lead to the symbolic system, but *further* cognitive development is likely to be different. We are not surprised, then, that as the unschooled Wolof children become older, some of them achieve conservation of quantity (in terms of the particular task given in the experiment) but that between the ages of 9 and 13 years the direction further development takes (again in terms of the particular "conservation task" of the experiment) is no longer the same: The meshing of the spontaneous cognitive activity of the child into the preexisting symbolic systems of mathematics and science does not take place.

For closer analysis we have chosen only one of the studies reported in the book by Bruner and associates. We could have used several other studies from that book (studies of Mexican and Eskimo children, further studies of Wolof children) employing different indexes of cognitive development (the use of color as against form for grouping, the use of superordinate categories supplied by language, the importance of syntax to grouping and concept formation) to make the same point. It should not be thought that the cognitive development of children in *different* preliterate societies is always identical; there are variations there too, and one of the errors into which we are only too liable to fall is to overlook those differences. Nevertheless, in regard to the contrast we have been highlighting, the other studies bear out our main argument. Greenfield, Reich, and Olver, summing up the results of their studies, state:

Schooling seems to be the single most powerful factor in stimulating abstraction. . . . With respect to the growth of representation, what turns out to be virtually impossible for the unschooled Wolofs are cognitive accomplishments that can be carried out *only* by symbolic means, for instance, nominal equivalence and superordinate language structures.[82]

The arguments presented here may seem to place undue emphasis on the impact of schooling on the development of the child. To gain perspective, let us remind ourselves of two points: We have been speaking about the effects on only *some* aspects of cognitive development, and we have been looking at studies of children in cultures where the Western-type school does indeed bring ways of looking at the world that are new, or partially new, to most of the people in that culture. In the Epilogue we shall open up some perspectives on education in our own technological society and at this point in historical time. This will give us the opportunity also to highlight the main points we have made throughout the book.

*Topics for
Further Exploration*

1. David McNeill, in *The Acquisition of Language* (New York: Harper & Row, 1970), pp. 20–23, gives some examples of the earliest speech utterances of children and makes the point that such utterances may be purely *expressive* (expressing a feeling) or *conative* (imperatives) but never purely *referential* (label or tag). How does this fit in with the definition of cognition given in this chapter? Now observe some children 1 to 2 years old and see whether you can confirm or refute McNeill's observation.

2. We have referred to nonverbal forms of communication both in
this chapter and in Chapters 2 and 4. What happens to nonverbal forms
of communication as the child gains better control of the verbal-linguistic
instrumentality? Observe some children aged 4, 6, and 10 years speaking
to each other about something that really concerns them and pay special
attention to body involvement. Observe also, if you can, deaf children
in a school for the deaf, from the youngest, with least language, to the
oldest, with most. Can you come up with any generalizations or with
ideas for research?

3. The ideas developed by Basil Bernstein concerning the relationship
between language, social class, and learning have been very influential
as a basis for developing compensatory-education programs for disadvantaged children. On the other hand, there has been much criticism of the
generalizations made from Bernstein's work as well as of the educational
implications, and much of this criticism has come from linguists. Read
W. Labov, *The Logic of Nonstandard English, Monograph Series on
Languages and Linguistics, 1969,* no. 22 (Washington, D.C.: Georgetown University School of Languages and Linguistics). What are *your*
conclusions?

References and Comments

1. L. S. Vygotsky, "Development of the Higher Mental Functions," in
    Psychological Research in the U.S.S.R., vol. 1 (Moscow: Progress
    Publishers, 1966), p. 43.

2. R. Carnap, *The Logical Syntax of Language* (London: Routledge &
    Kegan Paul, 1937).

3. This point has been made many times. Remy C. Kwant, in *Phenom-
    enology of Language* (Pittsburgh: Duquesne University Press,
    1965), devotes a whole chapter to "The Manifold Forms of
    Speech" in order to correct his own one-sidedness in the discussion
    of language and thought in a previous chapter. Bernard Kaplan,
    following Ombredane, distinguishes five functions of speech: affec-
    tive, ludic, practical, representative, and dialectical; it becomes
    evident that a philosopher like Carnap is concerned with only one
    of these—the dialectical usage—for this is how Kaplan defines the
    latter: "it is oriented towards the discovery of the rules immanent
    in the language or constructing artificial languages for specific
    functions. . . . The student of poetry, seeking to make explicit the

syntax of poetry, is also engaged in a dialectical activity" (*American Handbook of Psychiatry*, vol. 3, ed. S. Arieti [New York: Basic Books, 1966], chap. 41).

4. H. Werner and B. Kaplan, *Symbol Formation* (New York: Wiley, 1964), p. 24.

5. J. Church, *Three Babies: Biographies of Cognitive Development* (New York: Random House, 1966).

6. Referred to by M. Merleau-Ponty in *The Primacy of Perception* (Evanston, Ill.: Northwestern University Press, 1964), p. 123.

7. J. Piaget, *The Psychology of Intelligence* (London: Routledge & Kegan Paul, 1950).

8. E. Schachtel, *Metamorphosis* (New York: Basic Books, 1959), p. 33.

9. Erwin W. Straus, *Phenomenological Psychology: Selected Papers* (London: Tavistock Publications, 1966), p. 182.

10. Felix Krueger was the successor of Wilhelm Wundt at the University of Leipzig; the psychological "school" he founded became known as *Ganzheitspsychologie* (holistic psychology). While the Berlin Gestalt school associated with the names of Koffka, Köhler, and Wertheimer became very well known in North America, the Leipzig school did not, but it has had an influence nevertheless through the writings of Heinz Werner at Clark University. Werner specifically says of this influence: ". . . the Gestalt theory of the Leipzig school, in its stressing of pervasive feelings as the psycho-physiological background of all functioning, bears a relatively close relation to more recent organismic theories" (Werner and Kaplan, op. cit., p. 4n).

11. J. Church, *Language and the Discovery of Reality* (New York: Random House, 1961), p. 5.

12. Werner and Kaplan, op. cit., p. 68, say: "Most of these observers agree that the responses of a very young infant to visual stimuli cannot be considered indicative of a contemplative attitude— although such responses bear some superficial similarity to later contemplative behavior." According to Charlotte Bühler, as quoted by Werner and Kaplan, at 2 months an infant may often "stare through" rather than "look at" an object. Werner and Kaplan regard "acts of contemplation" as clearly discernible between 4 and 5 months of age.

13. According to Werner and Kaplan, op. cit., p. 91n., the notion of a schema dates back to formulations by the philosopher Kant in the eighteenth century. Werner pointed out the importance of the notion

for developmental psychology in a paper in 1912 ("Skizze zu einer Begriffstafel auf genetischer Grundlage," *Archiv für systematische Philosophie* 18:47–62). In 1934 R. d'Allonnes discussed the concept in "La Schematisation," in *Nouveau Traite de Psychologie*, vol. IV, ed. G. Dumas (Paris: Alcan). The concept plays an important part in Werner's developmental psychology and especially in Piaget's views on cognitive development.

14. Church, *Language and the Discovery of Reality*, op. cit., pp. 36–37.
15. For a review of Harlow's notion of "learning to learn," see McV. Hunt, *Intelligence and Experience* (New York: Ronald, 1961), pp. 77–83. On deprivation studies, see D. O. Hebb, *A Textbook of Psychology* (Philadelphia: Saunders, 1958), chap. 6.
16. L. Frank, *The Importance of Infancy* (New York: Random House, 1966), p. 88.

    H. W. Magoun, *The Waking Brain* (Springfield, Ill.: C. C. Thomas, 1963).

17. Church, *Three Babies*, op. cit., p. 168.
18. Ibid., p. 112.
19. Church, *Language and the Discovery of Reality*, op. cit., p. 61.
20. M. M. Lewis, *Language, Thought, and Personality* (London: Harrap, 1962).

    A. R. Luria, "The Directive Function of Speech in Development and Dissolution," *Word*, 15 (1959):341–464.

    A brief paper by Luria appears in *Readings in the Psychology of Cognition*, eds. R. C. Anderson and D. H. Ausubel (New York: Holt, Rinehart & Winston, 1965).

21. Church, *Three Babies*, op. cit., p. 44.
22. L. S. Vygotsky, *Thought and Language* (Cambridge, Mass.: M.I.T. Press, 1962).
23. J. Piaget, *Language and Thought of the Child* (London: Routledge & Kegan Paul, 1926). First published in French, 1923.
24. Problem solving at a perceptual and manipulative level was studied as a form of thinking by André Rey, *L'Intelligence Pratique Chez l'Enfant* (Paris: Universitaire Française, 1934). *Sensorimotor intelligence* is the term used by Piaget to describe the prelanguage "thinking" of the child.
25. The term *egocentric* has led to much confusion. In their book *Symbol Formation*, op. cit., p. 321, Werner and Kaplan say it appears that Vygotsky "misconstrued Piaget's concept of 'egocentrism' as descriptive of an asocial attitude," and they suggest that "Piaget's term

'egocentric' does not refer to asocial behavior but pertains rather to an early form of socialization." Whether this is what Piaget "really meant" or not, it is not what Piaget explicitly said. The basic difficulty lies in the choice of the label "egocentric." To the infant and the small child, it is self-evident that expression, whether in language or otherwise, may "communicate." There is no reason for the child to distinguish between "ego" and "other," "subject" and "object," "inner" and "outer"; these are distinctions he only gradually learns to make, as Piaget himself points out. The primary basis of all communication is contact, being with the other, and communication with the other and mutual understanding are *implicit* and are mediated by nonverbal means predominantly. Cf. also Chapter 4, on the total communication process out of which language becomes differentiated. It is only as the "ego" develops—i.e., as the child becomes more and more aware of its own *separate* identity in relation to others—that contact with the other no longer implies self-evident understanding; increasingly, then, communication takes the form of language, which articulates and specifies and helps reduce the "misunderstanding." The developmental sequence seems to be (and this is entirely in line with Werner's principle of progressive differentiation) from global and diffuse communication to more clearly articulated communication as the ego develops. To speak of "egocentric speech" at a stage when the ego is still poorly developed positively invites misunderstanding. If, as Werner and Kaplan maintain, "egocentric" speech refers to speech at an early level of socialization, the term is in fact redundant and should be dropped altogether; in addition, it is unnecessarily theory laden.

26. Vygotsky, op. cit., p. 16.
27. Ibid., pp. 19–20.
28. R. Brown, *Social Psychology* (New York: Free Press, 1965), pp. 344–348.
29. D. H. Russell, *Children's Thinking* (Boston: Ginn, 1956), especially pp. 155–164.
30. W. Stern, *Psychologie der frühen Kindheit*, 9th ed. (Heidelberg: Quelle und Meyer, 1967). This is one of the classical texts in the history of child psychology. The first edition appeared in 1914, an English translation of the third edition (*Psychology of Early Childhood*) in 1924 (London: Allen and Unwin).
31. D. Katz and R. Katz, *Gespräche mit Kindern. Untersuchungen zur Sozialpsychologie und Pädagogik* (Berlin: Springer, 1928).

32. J. S. Bruner et al., *Studies in Cognitive Growth* (New York: Wiley, 1966), p. 8.

33. M. Merleau-Ponty, *The Primacy of Perception* (Evanston, Ill.: Northwestern University Press, 1964), pp. 108–111.

34. See, e.g., E. T. Gendlin, *Experiencing and the Creation of Meaning* (Glencoe, Ill.: Free Press, 1962). Gendlin was associated for many years with Carl Rogers, the well-known "client-centered" therapist, and his interest in the fundamental problem of the relationship between individual experiencing and the articulation of experience in language arose from observing patients in psychotherapy.

35. It is a well-known fact that in North America the reaction to Sputnik was to place far more emphasis on intellectual achievement in schools than had been done in the preceding era and to become highly critical of Progressive Education, with its emphasis on emotional, social, and "total" personality development. One of the reasons (though surely there are others as well—Piaget is undoubtedly an ingenious experimenter providing rich experimental data and challenging theory) why American psychologists suddenly, and then increasingly, turned to the study of the Swiss psychologist Piaget appears to be that his interest is almost exclusively in the sort of cognitive development that leads to the modes of thinking required in mathematics, physics, and logic—in other words, ways of thinking required for progress in the natural sciences. However, we find this emphasis on the scientific ways of thinking not only in America but throughout the Western world. Kwant, *Phenomenology of Language*, op. cit., pp. 238–239, writes: "After a first rudimentary training at home, the school becomes the main factor in the formation of our children. This educational institution is primarily geared to rational knowledge, to the development of theoretical reason. In many countries the child's affectivity and emotionality, its bodily development, sportiveness and artistic inclinations are not sufficiently taken into consideration. Many people are now becoming aware of this one-sidedness, but relatively little is done to overcome it."

36. M. Merleau-Ponty, *The Phenomenology of Perception* (London: Routledge and Kegan Paul, 1962) distinguishes between *practognosis* (knowledge in action or thinking in action) and *gnosis* (knowledge—i.e., knowledge in contemplation).

37. B. Bernstein, "Social Structure, Language, and Learning," *Educational Research* 3 (1961):163–176. Either this, or one of his other papers on the same theme, is included in many of the books of

readings published in the 1960s—a clear reflection of the significance attributed to the ideas he developed. A great deal of the North American research on "culturally deprived" or "educationally disadvantaged" children, on which there exists a vast literature published in the 1960s, takes Bernstein's analysis of language in the different social classes as a starting point. See, e.g., Martin Deutsch, "The Role of Social Class in Language Development and Cognition," *American Journal of Orthopsychiatry* 35 (1966):78–88; and R. Hess and V. Shipman, "Early Experience and the Socialization of Cognitive Modes," *Child Development* 36 (1965):869–886. A similar analysis of the differences between the language of children from different social classes, with discussion of the implications for children's development, had already been given by Ph. Kohnstamm and M. J. Langeveld in Holland by about 1930; see M. J. Langeveld, *Taal en denken* (Groningen: J. B. Wolters, 1934). This work, however, did not become known in the English-speaking world. It is only after World War II, when in England the problem of "equal educational opportunity" for children from all social classes began to be tackled seriously and in North America the sociopolitical problems of poverty (particularly Negro) came to be faced, that the role of language deprivation, along with other forms of deprivation, became a central area of concern in research on cognitive development. For a powerful critique, not so much of Bernstein himself as of some compensatory education practices based on his analyses, see William Labov, *The Logic of Non-standard English*. Monograph Series on Languages and Linguistics, no. 22 (Washington, D.C.: Georgetown University School of Languages and Linguistics, 1969).

38. Less attention is paid to speaking about what constitutes good and bad behavior. The lower-class child learns little through speech—neither about values nor about himself nor about language.

39. For the first 4 to 6 years, the children from such groups may even do as well as other children or better, but then their performance drops off markedly; this pattern of performance has been referred to as the *crossover phenomenon*—see John F. Bryde, *The Sioux Indian Student: A Study of Scholastic Failure* (Pine Ridge, S.D.: Holy Rosary Mission), copyright by Rev. John Francis Bryde, 1966. This is in contrast to the *cumulative deficit phenomenon*, which appears to be more common.

40. Whether or not thought naturally tends toward logic, there are, as is widely recognized today, many logics. Cf. the statements made

in a discussion of Piaget's model of cognitive development: "A logic is a formal construction of a human being historically evolved, and there are many logics." "In other words, there is an historical evolution of logic. It is not a given quality of the human physiology. It is a product of human history and of the development of social man. There is nothing more social than logic" (M. Garrison, ed., *Cognitive Models and Development in Retardation, Monograph Supplement to American Journal of Mental Deficiency* 7 (January 1966):98.

41.   There are really two separate issues here: (a) differences in genetic endowment—we cannot doubt the existence of such differences, however difficult it may be to determine in any particular case what weight to assign to the genetic factor. See P. E. Vernon, *Intelligence and Attainment Tests* (London: University of London Press, 1960); *Intelligence and Cultural Environment* (London: Methuen, 1969); and A. Anastasi, *Differential Psychology* (New York: Macmillan, 1958). (b) biological maturation v. learning—e.g., as Eric Lenneberg has shown (*The Biological Basis of Language* [New York: Holt, Rinehart & Winston, 1968]), all normal children in every social class and in every culture learn to speak at "roughly" the same age, and in the acquisition of language all children pass through a "naming" phase before they form sentences of two words or more. The ability to acquire language and speech is species-specific; only human beings have "language"; it requires only minimal "releasers" from the social environment to trigger language acquisition. But Lenneberg is careful to point out that the numerous findings on social-class differences are not contradicted by the view he is setting out in his book (p. 136). What we are maintaining, then, is that, given a biological basis for language and cognition, and allowing for differences in genetic potentiality, human beings do not necessarily develop their modes of thinking in the direction regarded as normal in the educated classes of Western technological culture. Nor can we predict now what modes of thinking human beings in our culture will still develop in the future—cf. the theme of Marshall MacLuhan's writings, which is that the impact of modern mass-communication methods is gradually but profoundly changing our ways of perceiving and interpreting reality (see M. MacLuhan, *Understanding Media: The Extensions of Man* [London: Sphere, 1967] and *Gutenberg Galaxy* [London: Routledge and Kegan Paul, 1967]).

42. J. S. Bruner, "The Growth of Mind," *American Psychologist* 20 (1965):1007–1017.

43. John Gay and Michael Cole, *The New Mathematics and an Old Culture: a Study of Learning Among the Kpelle of Liberia* (New York: Holt, Rinehart & Winston, 1967).

44. D. R. Olson, *Cognitive Development: The Child's Acquisition of Diagonality* (New York and London: Academic, 1970).

45. C. Ramphal, "An Investigation into the Performance of Indian Children in Intelligence and Scholastic Tests in Relation to Delayed entrance to School" (Project III of Ph.D. thesis, "A Study of Three Current Problems of Indian Education," Department of Educational Psychology, University of Natal, South Africa, 1961).

46. W. H. O. Schmidt, "Socio-economic Status, Schooling, Intelligence, and Scholastic Progress in a Community in Which Education is not yet Compulsory," *Paedagogica Europaea* 2 (1966):275–289.

47. W. H. O. Schmidt and A. Nzimande, "Cultural Differences in Color/Form Preference and in Classificatory Behavior," *Human Development* 13 (1970): 140–148.

48. Gay and Cole, op. cit., p. 53.

49. Ibid., p. 53.

50. Ibid., p. 53.

51. Ibid., p. 54.

52. Ibid., p. 54.

53. Ibid., p. 54.

54. Ibid., p. 83.

55. For the difference between logical abstraction and psychological abstraction, see *Psychologie und Pädagogik*, eds. M. J. Langeveld, in Joseph Derbolav and Heinrich Roth (Heidelberg: Quelle und Meyer, 1959), pp. 68–73.

56. Gay and Cole, op. cit., p. 90.

57. Ibid., p. 20.

58. Ibid., p. 18.

59. Ibid., pp. 18, 20.

60. Ibid., p. 89.

61. E. Schachtel in *Metamorphosis—On the Development of Affect, Perception, Attention, and Memory* (New York: Basic Books, 1959), gives excellent analyses of people's embeddedness in their social world and their fear of leaving the familiar. "To perceive things differently from the people one knows, parents *and* peers, can be one of the most frightening experiences" (p. 188). "Both

times it is the anxiety aroused by the pathlessness, the absence of the signposts of familiarity. This is one source of our anxiety of the unknown. The other . . . is the fear of isolation from the shared, sociocentric perspective, if not ridicule or ostracism by their fellow men" (p. 204).

62. Theodor Litt, *Naturwissenschaft und Menschenbildung*, 2d ed. (Heidelberg: Quelle und Meyer, 1954).

63. Freidrich Copei, *Der fruchtbare Moment im Bildungsprozess*, 4th ed. (Heidelberg: Quelle und Meyer, 1958).

64. See B. Gerner, ed., *Das exemplarische Prinzip*, 3d ed. (Darmstadt: Wissenschaftliche Buchgesellschaft, 1968).

    W. H. O. Schmidt, "Curriculum and Method in the Academic High School: Some Fundamental Considerations," *International Review of Education* 8 (1962–1963): 344–355.

    M. Wagenschein, "Zum Begriff des exemplarischen Lernens," *Zeitschrift fur Pädagogik* 2 (1956).

65. L. Festinger, *Conflict, Decision, and Dissonance* (London: Tavistock, 1964).

66. D. E. Berlyne, *Conflict, Arousal, and Curiosity* (New York: McGraw-Hill, 1960).

67. Gay and Cole, op. cit., p. 16.

68. M. H. Watkins, "The West African 'Bush' School," in *Education and Culture: Anthropological Approaches*, ed. G. D. Spindler (New York: Holt, Rinehart & Winston, 1964), pp. 426–443.

69. Gay and Cole, op. cit., p. 17.

70. See also Bruner, op. cit., pp. 1007–1017.

71. See J. Piaget, "Nécessité et Signification des Recherches Comparatives en Psychologie Génétique," *International Journal of Psychology* 1 (1966):3–13.

    R. E. Ripple and V. N. Rockcastle, eds., *Piaget Rediscovered* (Ithaca, N. Y.: Cornell University Press, 1964).

    R. H. Ojemann and Karen Pritchett, eds., *Giving Emphasis to Guided Learning* (Denver: Denver University Press, 1966).

Piaget stresses that cognitive development is not merely a matter of biological (physiological, neurological) maturation; he is known to react angrily to the charge that he holds such a naive view. Instead he stresses the child's interaction with—assimilation of and accommodation to—the environment and the continuous process of *equilibration* (i.e., the continuous upsetting and reestablishing of adaptation to the environment). This entails successive restructurings of the total cognitive structure of the child, until the end-point toward which everything tends is reached: the stage of *formal operations* or sustained *propositional thinking* attained during adolescence and adulthood. In the stage of formal operations, we readily recognize the ideal of the thinker in modern mathematics and logic. But does all thinking tend toward this? Under what conditions does it do so? Piaget insists that "learning" and "teaching" have little or nothing to do with the emergence of new and changed cognitive structures—exposure to an environment, involving assimilation and accommodation, yes; learning and teaching, no. If he were merely warning against the ever-present danger of mere verbalism and rote learning, his point would be well taken—and indeed the protagonists of the "discovery method" of learning and teaching like to appeal to the authority of Piaget for support (see Ripple and Rockcastle, and Ojemann and Pritchett, especially the paper and discussion by Kohnstamm). But Piaget's views seem to imply more: that given an environment with which to interact and suitable conditions to encourage acting and reacting (assimilating and accommodating), the ways of thinking required in mathematics, logic, and science will *inevitably* emerge. The directive and guiding function of the teacher, channeling the thinking of the child and giving or suggesting to him preformed ways of processing information and interpreting reality (preformed by creative thinkers in the past), is either denied or so played down as to be insignificant.

72. Gay and Cole, op. cit., p. 38.
73. Ibid., pp. 39, 40.
74. Schmidt and Nzimande, op. cit., pp. 140–148.
75. Bruner, op. cit.
76. See J. Piaget, *The Child's Conception of Number* (London: Routledge & Kegan Paul, 1952). First French ed., 1941. A simple, lucid description and discussion is given by Wohlwill in "The Mystery of the Prelogical Child," *Psychology Today* 1 (1967):24–34.
77. Bruner, op. cit., p. 235.
78. See note 55.
79. Zimiles speaks of a *prenumerical* concept of quantity. See H. Zimiles, "A Note on Piaget's Concept of Conservation," *Child Development* 34 (1963):691–695.
80. L. von Bertallanfy, *Minds, Robots, and Men* (New York: Braziller, 1967).

We never have reality in itself, only perspectives on it; it is the theorist, the scientist, and the poet who grind the lenses through which we see reality.

81. Because, under the impact of modern science and the stress on the objectivity of science, psychologists have tended to elevate scientific-ally conceived "reality" into the only reality, phenomenological psychologists have stressed the importance of the "lived world," the naive, prescientific experiencing that does not lose its significance as a result of science; on the contrary, it remains basic to man's behavior. For a fundamental treatment of this issue, see Merleau-Ponty, *The Phenomenology of Perception*, and E. Straus, *The Primary World of Senses* (Glencoe, Ill.: Free Press, 1963).

   For a review of the literature and an interesting series of experiments in this field, see Bruce Bain, "Toward a Theory of Perception: Participation as a Function of Body-Flexibility" (Ph.D. Dissertation, University of Alberta, Edmonton [Canada], 1970). To appear in *Journal of General Psychology*.

82. Bruner, op. cit., pp. 317, 318.

Epilogue

The whole teaching-and-learning continuum, which was once tied in an orderly and productive way to the passing of generations and the growth of the child into a man—this whole process has exploded in our faces.[1]

Margaret Mead

We have been concerned with placing the study of child development in a human, cultural, and educational context. In doing so we have not disregarded the biological-evolutionary context. Indeed, we have asserted that two species-specific characteristics of *Homo sapiens* are basic to the conceptual framework within which to view child development: man as symbolizer and the child as a being that *must* be educated in order to realize his potentialities as a human being.

In looking at man the symbolizer, we have paid special attention to language. What we were most concerned with was not merely to see the acquisition of language as a discrete series of events but to see the implications of these events for every other aspect of the child's relationship to the world and to himself.

In speaking about the child as a being that must be educated, we defined education as an interactive process between an educator (adult) and an educand (child), irrespective of the institutional setting in which this interaction takes place. *Schooling* was seen as a subset of *education*, and we looked at the impact of the Western-type school from a scientific-technological culture on the cognitive development of children in cultures other than our own. We now end by referring briefly to our own schools, at this point in time.

The Western-type school we have described as the socializing agent of our own technologically oriented society. Where this socializing agent is transplanted (even if with suitable modifications) to a predominantly nontechnological society such as in developing countries, the school does indeed teach the child to think in a new way. In our own society it is not so much a *new* way of thinking, which only the school can teach, as an extension and further development of ways of thinking that have already begun. There are exceptions, and we referred to one of these when we dealt with social-class differences in relation to what the school is trying to teach.

We should, therefore, have an ideal situation: the school extending and expanding what the child has already experienced, knows, and can do, and the experiences in school constantly reinforced by the experiences outside school. The reality, as we know, is different. Young people, many of them from the higher social class and including some of the most intelligent among their peers, are dropping out. The schools are under attack. In the introductory chapter we started by referring to the Industrial Revolution, which brought about changes in the conditions of life under which children grew up. What are the changed conditions under which children in our culture grow up now?

Mead, in the article from which the opening quotation is taken, makes a distinction between *vertical* and *lateral* transmission of knowledge. Vertical transmission is concerned with transmission "of the tried and the true by the old, mature, and experienced teachers to the young, immature, and inexperienced pupil." Lateral transmission "to every sentient member of society, of what has been discovered, invented, created, manufactured, or marketed." The words used by Mead to describe lateral transmission probably reflect the fact that she was addressing herself to a business school audience, for much more is really meant by lateral transmission. The child's sources of information today are no longer confined to the parent, the priest, the schoolteacher. The communication media—newspapers, cinema, theater, radio, television above all—bring information not only about new discoveries, inventions, and marketable products but also about what is happening *to people* in all corners of the world.

It is one thing to know that a war is going on somewhere; it is another to see the destruction and human suffering before your very eyes, even though it be in the physical comfort of your living room. So it is also with poverty, racial riots, living conditions of people in remote areas, life in different cultures, and the hopes and frustrations of people from all walks of life and in all geographical areas of the world. We can refuse to think about and face the implications of these impressions, but we cannot erase them from our awareness. People who were once far away and concerned us only as part of a strange, strange world are now near, and we have to redefine our relationship to them and theirs to us. We have become, to use a now-hackneyed phrase, parts of a global village. The conditions under which children grow up have indeed changed. The implications of these changes are every bit as far-reaching—if not more so—as the changes brought about by the Industrial Revolution. Unfortunately, when we ourselves experience profound change around us, we are seldom able to see its implications clearly. How can the basic notions developed in this book shed light on the implications of these changes for our understanding of child and adolescent development at this stage in history?

The vertical transmission "of the tried and the true by the old, mature, and experienced teachers to the young, immature, and inexperienced pupil" may appear to be what we have been calling the interaction between educator and child. But this would be a gross misunderstanding. In our definition of the interaction between educator and educand, we have included the *reciprocity* in the relationship, the primordial *sharing* in the earliest stage, and the *coresponsive participation* of adult and child in a common world. It is true that the lateral transmission of knowledge on the vast scale made possible by modern technology has created an entirely new world, to which children are exposed very early in their lives. But it is a new world common to adults and children. They both have to come to terms with it.

When we take seriously the reciprocity involved in the relationship, there comes a time when it is not always clear who is educating whom: the old the young, or the young the old. The adult may be more experienced and mature, but the categories and symbolizations that have been formed on the basis of his past experiences in a world that was different may make his perception of what is happening now, under changed conditions, unduly selective. On the other hand, the young, having much less experience, may be much more open to experience of the world as it is now and in which they have to shape their own future. Often it is through them that the adult admits into his own awareness perceptions that do not fit his previous categorizations and judgments. Who, then, is educating whom?

We can also look at the relationship in a slightly different way. Eriksen describes ten stages in the development of the ego.[2] In our context we do not need to describe them all. It is sufficient to indicate the rationale underlying his thinking and then to say something of the stage that concerns us here—what he calls the *identity crisis* stage of adolescence. At each stage in the development of the child, there are certain tasks with which he has to learn to cope. From the first stage (up to the age of say, 2 years) there must emerge a feeling of basic trust in people. In the second stage he must develop autonomy. If he has not yet gained basic trust, he carries into the second stage a deficit. The third stage Eriksen sees as one in which the child is concerned with "industry"—with testing and expanding his skills. If he does not carry too many deficits from the previous two stages into this new stage, he should pass through it with his ego strengthened for what lies ahead. Not to cope fully with the demands of a particular stage does not doom the child to failure later, but it makes it more difficult for him.

It is the identity-crisis stage of adolescence that is of particular interest to us. Here the young person is asking: Who am *I*? What do *I* want? Am I what my parents and other adults see in me? What are *my* values? What do *I* really believe in? Are the values of the adults my values? The search for identity inevitably involves testing the values of the parents and of adults generally. If there has been reciprocity in the educational relationship all along, the adult will examine his own values and, as often as not, change in the process. Again we can ask: Who is educating whom?

We said in the introductory chapter that the educative relationship emerges out of a biological necessity but points to a realm of society and culture, which man has created. We can now say that, if the relationship has been one of reciprocity from the earliest beginnings, it finds its end and fulfillment in a human relationship in which the distinction between educator and educand falls away. They are now coresponsible for their society and their culture; they are on equal footing.

References

1. Margaret Mead, "Thinking Ahead: Why Is Education Obsolete?" *Harvard Business Review* 36 (November-December 1958).
2. E. Erikson, *Childhood and Society*, 2d ed. (New York: Norton, 1963).

Bibliography

I. Basic Theoretical Approaches

Baldwin, A. L. *Theories of Development.* New York: Wiley, 1967.

Comprehensive, descriptive, evaluative—good for becoming aware of a wide range of theoretical stances; not a substitute for reading some of the writings of the theorists themselves.

Langer, J. *Theories of Development.* New York: Holt, Rinehart & Winston, 1969.

A slim volume. Does not give the ideas of any one theorist in detail, but groups theories according to their underlying assumptions and style: psychoanalytically oriented (e.g., Eriksen), organic-lamp theories (e.g., Piaget, Heinz Werner), mechanical-mirror theories (generally based on modern North American learning theories). Langer's own preference shines through clearly.

II. Systematic Description of Child Development from Birth to Adolescence

Mussen, P. H.; Conger, J. J.; and Kagan, J. *Child Development and Personality,* 3d ed. (New York: Harper & Row, 1969).

Comprehensive review, empirical, eclectic in its theoretical orientation. The third edition differs considerably from prevous editions: More attention is paid to the ideas and research of cognitive psychologists. Has a companion volume by the same authors, *Readings in Child Development and Personality,* 2d ed. (New York: Harper & Row, 1970), which contains an excellent selection of research papers.

Stone, L. J., and Church, J. *Childhood and Adolescence: A Psychology of the Growing Person,* 2d ed. New York: Random House, 1968.

Emphasis on description and interpretation. Reads very well.

III. The Child in Historical Perspective

Aries, P. *Centuries of Childhood: A Social History of Family Life.* New York: Knopf, 1962.

Original in French. A fascinating study of how children were seen in former centuries, what was expected of them, and the relationships between social conditions and child development.

Berg, J. H. van den. *The Changing Nature of Man: Introduction to a Historical Psychology.* New York: Norton, 1961.

Original in Dutch. Analyzes the changes that have taken place in the conditions under which children grow up, from the eighteenth century to the present—actual social and economic conditions, and the adult image of the child. Has some challenging and controversial propositions.

Kessen, W., ed. *The Child.* New York: Wiley, 1965.

Kessen is at Yale. A selection of readings from the eighteenth century to the present day, with quite lengthy interpretations by Kessen.

Wishy, B. *The Child and the Republic: The Dawn of Modern American Child Nurture.* Philadelphia: University of Pennsylvania Press, 1968.

As the subtitle indicates, the book looks at ideas and practices regarding the rearing of children in North America in a historical perspective.

Reading one or more of these books is a good antidote to what you read under I and II—it could lead you to asking quite new questions about child development, and it may be more fun.

IV. Language and Cognition in Child Development

Church, J. *Three Babies: Biographies of Cognitive Development.* New York: Random House, 1966.

Naturalistic observation of infant development. A great deal of information that requires interpretation. Could be a basis for interesting discussion.

————. *Language and the Discovery of Reality.* New York: Random House, 1966.

A cognitive developmental psychology that opens up perspectives on language and cognition but also on much more.

Lewis, M. M. *Language, Thought, and Personality.* London and New York: Harraps and Basic Books, 1963.

Traces development from its beginnings to middle childhood, with emphasis on the interrelationships between language, thought, and personality. Lewis is in England. He writes simply and very coherently, with little technical jargon. He is particularly good in interpreting some of Piaget's ideas relating to language in middle childhood.

McNeill, D. *The Acquisition of Language*. New York: Harper & Row, 1970.

One of a group of so-called developmental psycholinguists, strongly influenced by Chomsky, who have been very active since 1964 and are all coming out with books now. The basic issues they raise are a challenge to much of our thinking about development.

Menyuk, Paula. *The Acquisition and Development of Language*. Cambridge, Mass.: M.I.T. Press, 1971.

Same comment as for McNeill.

Slobin, D. *Psycholinguistics*. Glenview, Ill.: Scott, Foresman, 1971.

Same comment as for previous two. Slobin's book is perhaps the easiest and quickest to read.

Smith, F., and Miller, G. A., eds. *The Genesis of Language*. Cambridge, Mass.: M.I.T. Press, 1966.

Contains the papers and discussions of the 1964 conference that started the current ferment in developmental psycholinguistics.

Werner, H., and Kaplan, B. *Symbol Formation*. New York: Wiley, 1963.

This book places the symbolizing activity of the human being (not just language) at the center of its interpretation of human development. Perhaps we should take a comment from another commentator: to be read early in the morning, when you're fresh, but a must for any serious student of language—and, we would add, development.

Flavell, D. H. *The Developmental Psychology of Jean Piaget*. New York: Van Nostrand Reinhold, 1963.

For many years this was the definitive book for informing oneself on the overall work of Piaget.

Furth, H. *Piaget and Knowledge: Theoretical Foundations*. Englewood Cliffs, N.J.: Prentice-Hall, 1969.

The most informed treatment of Piaget the theorist, by a man who really knows the philosophical tradition within which Piaget must be seen.

Luria and Yudovich. *Speech and the Development of Mental Processes in the Child*. London: Staples Press, 1959.

An experiment with a pair of twins—detailed analysis of development in speech, play, intellectual activities, and their interrelationships. A Russian study showing the influence of Vygotsky's ideas.

Olson, D. *Cognitive Development*. New York: Academic, 1970.

The book has the subtitle *The Acquisition of Diagonality*, and it is the investigation of this specific problem that gradually leads the author into building a whole theory of cognitive development. An important book giving a reinterpretation of some of Piaget's notions.

Piaget, J. Too numerous to mention—see references in Flavell and Baldwin's books.

Attention should, however, be paid to his earliest book, *The Language and Thought of the Child* (paperback), because many of the basic issues are raised there already—see particularly his prefaces to different editions.

Vygotsky, L. S. *Language and Thought.* Cambridge, Mass.: M.I.T. Press, 1962. Also in paperback.

If you haven't read this yet, your education has been neglected. The papers contained in the book were first published (in Russian) as early as the 1920s and 1930s.

V. Cross-Cultural Perspectives in Child Development

Ainsworth, Mary D. *Infancy in Uganda.* Baltimore, Md.: Johns Hopkins Press, 1967.

An important study that also refers to many other studies in this area.

Bronfenbrenner, U. *Two Worlds of Childhood: U.S. and U.S.S.R.* New York: Russell Sage, 1970.

A study in contrasts, giving much food for thought.

Bruner, J. S., and associates. *Studies in Cognitive Growth.* New York: Wiley, 1966.

Contains a number of studies of Wolof, Mexican, and Eskimo children that raise important issues about how we conceptualize development.

Gay, J., and Cole, M. *The New Mathematics in an Old Culture: A Study of Learning Among the Kpelle in Liberia.* New York: Holt, Rinehart & Winston, 1967.

Contains a lot of data and observations that are important to understanding development.

Ihsan, A., and Dennis, W., eds. *Cross-Cultural Studies of Behavior.* New York: Holt, Rinehart & Winston, 1970.

A collection of papers giving an idea of the range of problems being investigated.

Mead, Margaret. *Coming of Age in Samoa.* New York: Morrow, 1928. Now available in paperback.

————. *Growing Up in New Guinea.* New York: Morrow, 1930. Now available in paperback.

These two books are a study in contrasts between two preliterate societies.

Mead, Margaret, and Wolfenstein, Martha. *Childhood in Contemporary Cultures.* Chicago: University of Chicago Press, 1963.

Interesting studies of child rearing in Europe and North America.

Sears, R. R.; Maccoby, Eleanor E.; and Levin, H. *Patterns of Child Rearing.* New York: Harper & Row, 1957.

Vernon, P. E. *Intelligence and Cultural Environment.* London: Methuen, 1969.

Whiting, Beatrice B., ed. *Six Cultures: Studies of Child Rearing.* New York: Wiley, 1963.

Index

Abbreviation of language, 124, 125
Abstract concepts, 115, 153
Accommodation, 4
Acculturation, 7
Action space of infants, 112–113
Activity-affect expansion, 111
Adaptation, 49
Adolescence, 2, 168
Adult. *See also* Mother-child relationship
  relation to child, 39
Affect, 107
  and cognition, 113–115
Ainsworth, Mary D., 41n.
Alphabet, simplified, 10
Animal educandum, 20, 21
Animal psychology, 4
Animal symbolicum, 64
Anthropology of child, 41n.
Ape in Our House, The (Hayes), 23
Apes. *See also* Chimpanzees; Monkeys
  play ability, 24
  study of, 23–26
Aries, Philippe, 13n.–14n.
Assimilation, 4
Autonomy of child, 38–39, 40n.
Awareness. *See* Cognition

Bees, behaviorial studies, 71
Behavior
  coresponsive, 116–118
  and speech, 120–121
Behaviorism, 6, 121
Bellugi, Ursula, 76–79, 85n., 105
Benveniste, 71
Berlyne, D. E., 144
Bernstein, Basil, 101, 158n.–159n.
  on social class, 131–135
Betts, Emma A., 9
Biological influences, 3–5, 12–13, 65–66. *See also* Maturation
Body language, 107

Bowlby, John, 34
Brown, Roger, 33–34, 76–79, 85n., 105, 125, 129
Bruner, J. S., 10, 137, 148–149
Bühler, Karl, 4, 70

Carnap, R., 106
Cassirer, Ernst, 61, 70
  on rationality, 62–63, 64, 65
Centuries of Childhood (Aries), 13n.–14n.
Chase, R. A., 25
Child labor, 2, 13n., 14n.
Chimpanzees
  emotions, 69
  sounds, 69
  study of, 4
Choice, 39
Church, Joseph, 40, 109–111, 113, 119
Class differences in language, 101
Classification, 147–148
Cognition
  and affect, 113–115
  and culture, 136–140
  defined, 106–109
  development, 109–110, 146–153
  early, 118–119
  rational, 135–136
Cognitive dissonance, 144
Cole, Michael, 49, 137–140, 144–145, 147
Communication, animal, 25–26. *See also* Language
  mother-child, 68
  nonverbal, 35, 36
  among preschool children, 122–123
Concentration, 90
Concept formation, 107, 129, 140–142
  and culture, 137–140
  scientific, 89–100

177